D1083443

ROSSIGNOL

An Edition and Translation

J. L. BAIRD and JOHN R. KANE

With Introductory Essay on the Nightingale Tradition

by J. L. Baird

The Kent State University Press

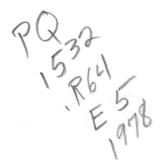

Permission has been granted by the British Library Board for an edition of
Rossignol, folios 34-38 of MS. Egerton 2834. The Board has also very gra-
ciously given permission for reproduction of the first folio of the *Rossignol* to
be used in this edition.

Contents

Acknowledgments

With the *Rossignol*, as with any scholarly work, innumerable debts of gratitude have accumulated, all of which, though remembered, could scarcely be acknowledged in detail. We would like, however, to express our special appreciation to the following friends and colleagues: Lorrayne Y. Baird, Associate Professor, Youngstown State University, for her usual perceptive and sound criticism; Garrett McCutchan, Instructor in Italian, Kent State University, for an early reading of the MS. and many helpful suggestions; Giuseppe Baglivi, Assistant Professor in Italian, Kent State University; Martin Nurmi, Professor of English, Kent State University; Paul Rohmann, Director, Kent State University Press; Mrs. Lee Stockdale, Administrative Assistant, English Department, Kent State University; Mrs. Hazel Young, Interlibrary Loan, Kent State University Library; and, finally, our two anonymous outside readers of the MS., for their constructive criticism. We are also grateful for the generous assistance of A. N. E. D. Schofield, Assistant Keeper of MSS., The British Library.

Rossignol

Entering Western literature as it does with Homer, the nightingale has an extremely long historical role to play in the vast expanse of European letters.[1] That fact in and of itself is not unusual, of course, since poets, by very nature of their craft, have always had a close affinity with such "warblers of the woodland wild." What does strike one as strange about this small, uncolorful, rather insignificant creature, however, is the remarkably varied and contradictory symbolic functions it has been called upon to fullfill. Its naturally quite neutral note has at one time or another, and indeed not infrequently during exactly the same historical period, symbolized the supreme, though perhaps unattainable, height of earthly joy and, on the other hand, the lowest depth of human misery and despair. Similarly, the bird has stood for the highest possible kind of love, *caritas*, Christian love directed toward God, while at the opposite extreme it has sung the ecstasies of purely sensuous, at times quite overtly lascivious, human love, with varying gradations between these two. Furthermore, and quite startlingly, it has been employed in military contexts, shrieking out at the enemy its warlike cry of "Kill, kill, kill." In the latter part of the thirteenth century, the Franciscan Friar John Peacham, in a remarkable feat of poetic creation, took up all of these various strands of the nightingale legends and wove all of them into the texture of his splendid religious poem, *Philomena praevia*.[2] Some time there-

---

1. At the outset of this Introduction it will be well to indicate my substantial indebtedness to three very fine articles devoted to the nightingale tradition. Even where I have enlarged upon their findings and gone beyond their immediate aims, or even where I have diverged markedly from their viewpoint, my debt will be quite clear to the reader. The articles are, in order of their importance for the present work: F. J. E. Raby, "Philomena praevia temporis amoeni," in *Mélanges*, ed. Joseph de Ghellinck (Gembloux: J. Duculot, 1951), II, 435-48; Thomas Alan Shippey, "Listening to the Nightingale," *Comparative Literature*, 22 (1970), 46-60; and Albert R. Chandler, "The Nightingale in Greek and Latin Poetry," *Classical Journal*, 30 (1934), 78-84.
2. Latin text in *Analecta Hymnica*, L, 602-16.

after another quite gifted poet, whose name has not come down to us, turned Peacham's sometimes harsh Latin into the softer, more mellifluous French of the medieval vernacular lyric tradition. It is this latter poem which herein receives its first modern edition, accompanied by a fairly literal prose translation.

The Tragic Theme

The dominant tradition of the nightingale in Antiquity, and I suppose in general the only nightingale tradition for the casual modern reader of classical literature, was one of heavy sadness, sorrow, tragedy, and death. It is, of course, a result of the powerful influence of Homer and Ovid that this particular theme—one of many even in Antiquity—became so pervasive in the post-Classical era, especially from the Renaissance forward. Yet, as is seldom remembered, each of these poets, in fact, recounted a significantly differing version of a single basic myth.[3] In this realm, obviously, the song of the bird is always melancholy, mournful, *querulus*. This sadly beautiful note makes its first appearance in the *Odyssey*. Weighed down by grief and care over the long-delayed return of Odysseus to Ithaca, Penelope listens in her sorrow to the plaintive cries of the nightingale in the early spring, and like the notes of the bird her thoughts turn hither and yon:

> But to me has a god given sorrow that is beyond all measure, for day by day I find my joy in mourning and lamenting, while looking to my household tasks and those of my women in the house, but when night comes and sleep lays hold of all, I lie upon my bed, and sharp cares, crowding close about my throbbing heart, disquiet me, as I mourn. Even as when the daughter of Pandareus, the nightingale of the greenwood, sings sweetly, when spring is newly come, as she sits perched amid the thick leafage of the trees, and with many trilling notes pours forth her rich voice in wailing for her child, dear Itylus, whom she had one

---

3. Robert Graves, for example, does not even allude to Homer's version, although he lists the *Odyssey* as a source, incorrectly, as it turns out, as XIX. 418 rather than the proper XIX.518ff. See *The Greek Myths*, two vols. (Baltimore: Penguin Books, 1955), Sect. 46.

day slain with the sword unwittingly, Itylus, the son of king Zethus; even so my heart sways to and fro in doubt. . . .[4]

This undetailed, symbolically allusive story is clearly not the most widely known one of sex and horror, which has so fully permeated Western literature. Homer's is a simpler, though still violent form, deriving ultimately from a version in which a mother, seeking to murder some other woman's son, mistakenly kills her own, is then changed into a nightingale, and sorrowfully bewails her loss ever after. The most influential version, however, is the familiar one of rape, mutilation, murder, and cannibalism. And though apparently Greek in origin, its widespread popularity in post-Classical times stems from the Latin form that it received at the hands of Ovid. In brief, Ovid's version is as follows:

Tereus marries Procne, from which union is born a son, Itys. Procne persuades Tereus to bring her sister Philomela to Thrace for a visit. At first sight of Philomela, however, Tereus is engulfed in the flames of lust, "like fire in the white grain, dry leaves, or the hay stored in the barns."

He brings Philomela back to Thrace and there viciously rapes, imprisons, and mutilates her by cutting out her tongue. Philomela manages to inform Procne of her plight by weaving her story in a tapestry which she contrives to smuggle out of the prison. Procne then frees her sister, and the two take savage revenge by killing, cooking, and serving up Tereus' own son Itys to him at a feast. When they take their wildly demented revenge by informing Tereus that he has just devoured his own child, Tereus chases the two with his sword, until, just as he is about to catch them, all three are metamorphosed into birds.[5]

---

4. Homer, *The Odyssey*, trans. E. V. Rieu (Baltimore: Penguin Books, 1946), p. 301, XIX.518-24. Penelope is actually speaking to Odysseus himself, whom she has not yet recognized.

5. *Metamorphoses* VI.424-674. The particular bird each is transformed into varies in the different traditions. Ovid mentions specifically only the Hoopoe (Tereus), though it is generally assumed that his Philomela is changed into a nightingale—*philomela* becomes, after all, the common noun for nightingale in Latin—and Procne into a swallow. In some versions, however, it is Philomela who becomes a swallow; Procne, a nightingale. This is the tradition, strangely, that Dante follows; see Purgatorio IX.13-15 and XVII.19-21. The form *Philomela*, by normal linguistic process, will later show up as *Philomena* or *Filomena*, forms which will be used herein without further comment.

[3]

Although in direct opposition, as we shall see, to the view of a joyous nightingale, this is the most widely known and frequently repeated version in antique, as well as modern, literature. Its universal popularity in Antiquity is probably to be attributed, as Chandler believes, to the influence of Sophocles through his tragedy *Tereus*, a work which unfortunately has come down to us only in fragmentary form.[6]

As might be expected, it is the tradition of the grief-stricken nightingale that Vergil knows, although he, alone among the ancients, fully rationalizes the cause of the sorrows in his beautiful lyric lament:

> Qualis populea maerens Philomela sub umbra
> Amissos queritur fetus, quos durus arator
> Observans nido implumis detraxit: at illa
> Flet noctem; ramoque sedens miserabile carmen
> Integrat et maestis late loca questibus implet.[7]
>
> [Georgics, IV. 511-15]

How Philomela, grieving under the shadows of the poplars, laments for her lost little ones, whom some crude plowboy has carried off unfledged from the nest: she weeps throughout the night; and sitting on her bough, she continually reiterates her sorrowful song and fills all the wide fields with her plaints.[8]

This bird of sorrows is known, of course, to the Middle Ages. It could hardly be otherwise, since both Vergil and Ovid exerted such a powerful influence over the whole range of the period. But, in its pure Ovidian form certainly, it no longer plays a dominant, nor even, comparatively speaking, a very important role. Its voice is heard, for example, sporadically, but only sporadically, in the Latin spring/love songs of the high Middle Ages, beginning about the twelfth century. And recognizable in these lyrics only by the persisting verb *queror*

---

6. See Albert R. Chandler, "The Nightingale in Greek and Latin Poetry," *Classical Journal*, 30 (1934), 79. Also Pauly-Wissowa, *Real-Encyclopädie der Classischen Altertumswissenschaft*, under *Philomela*.

7. Vergil does, however, make use, even later in the *Georgics*, of the other version. See *Georgics* IV.15ff. and *Bucolics* VI.78.

8. Unless otherwise indicated, this and all other translations are by Professor Kane and myself.

and adjective forms *querens, querula,* the ancient tradition, in point of fact, frequently seems strangely at odds with the light and joyous context in which it occurs. The following lyric from the famous *Carmina Burana,* quoted in full to give the full flavor of the context, illustrates the point well:

Musa venit carmine,
dulci modulamine:
pariter cantemus,
ecce virent omnia,
prata, rus et nemus,
mane garrit alaudula,
lupilulat cornicula,
iubente natura
philomena queritur
antiqua de iactura.

Hirundo iam finsat,
cignus dulce trinsat
memorando fata,
cuculat et cuculus
per nemora vernata.

Pulchre canunt volucres,
nitet terre facies
vario colore,
et in partum solvitur
redolens odore.

Late pandit tilia
frondes, ramos, folia,
thymus est sub ea,
viridi cum gramine,
in quo fit chorea.

Patet et in gramine
iocundo rivus murmure.
locus est festivus,
ventus cum temperie
susurrat tempestivus.[9]

The singer comes with a song, with a sweet melody: let us all
sing like that. Look, all things grow green again: the meadow,
the fields, the wood. The lark chatters in the morning, the young
crows cry out their caws, all so naturally. Philomena com-
plains of her ancient wrong. Now the swallow chatters; sweetly
the swan twitters, in tune with nature's law, and the cuckoo
calls out through the leafy wood. All the birds sing sweetly; the
face of the earth shines forth multicolored and exudes its sweet
perfume. The linden tree spreads abroad its leafy branches.
Thyme and the green grass beneath the tree provide a perfect
place for dancing. A happy little brook murmurs past; a soft
wind whispers in the glade. This is a joyous, delightful place!

In the beautiful Latin lyric *Dum Diane vitrea*, once attributed
to Abelard, Philomena again *querens canit*, but only in a con-
text that moves immediately into the sweet playing "in
gramine cum virgine speciosa," followed by the delightful
drowsy satiety which comes after "defessa Veneris com-
mercia."[10] Significant too are the lines from *Axe Phoebus aureo*:

Philomena querule
Terea retractat,
dum canendo merule
carmina coaptat.[11]

9. For easily accessible texts with translations, see Helen Waddell,
Mediaeval Latin Lyrics (New York: Henry Holt & Co., 1948), pp. 238-40; George
F. Whicher, *The Goliard Poets* (New York: New Directions Books, 1949), pp.
196-97.

10. For texts with translations, see Waddell, pp. 264-67; also, Whicher,
pp. 30-35.

11. Whicher, p. 42. Whicher translates "Sad Philomel for once abates
her tale of Terean wrong." But if Philomena has given up her *querule* and is
imitating the blackbird, "sad" seems a strange addition to the text. Also,
surely *Terea* of the Latin text is intended as the bird's cry. See Graves [I.166]
for meaningful representations of the bird's cry in antiquity. Also see section

Philomena retracts her complaining cry, "Terea," and imitates instead the (happy) song of the blackbird.

Only in such slight ways then, the ancient wrong remembered in simple, single words, does the sorrowing nightingale continue a rather tenuous existence in the seemingly alien environment of the Latin love lyrics. It is not to be thought, however, that the Classical tradition is, more or less, lost to the Middle Ages. Here in the relatively small compass of the love lyric, it has simply been overwhelmed, as we shall see, by the far more powerful tradition of a *leta*, "joyous," philomena. In larger, more expansive narrative contexts, the tale is recounted at length in all its physical horror. Yet even in these works, the story is not allowed to stand on its own merits: it is either, as was once the fashion to say, fully medievalized, that is, allegorized, or, in a much more interesting development, it is rather nervously, almost frantically, brought into adjustment, even after all the gory details, with the tradition of the light, joyous bird.

In the late thirteenth or early fourteenth century, the *Ovide moralisé* renders the full Ovidian form of the story, though with a few additional significant details, since, as the writer tells us at the beginning of his moralization, "De Philomena faut le conte,/Si com Crestiens le reconte" ("the story of Philomena as Chretien tells it was lacking some-

below, pages 18-23, on the meaning of *oci*. In this area George Gascoigne (16th century) wins the prize for ingenuity but also for absurdity in his enumeration and interpretation of nightingale cries, ranging from *Tereu, Tereu* (vocative of Tereus) to *Phy* (i.e., *fie*) to *jug*, interpreted as both *jugum* ([marriage] yoke) and *jugulator* (slayer) to *Nemesis*, etc. The following verses will illustrate well his prosaic literalness:

> So that it semes hir well,
> *Phy, phy, phy, phy,* to sing,
> Since *phy* befytteth him so well
> In every kind of thing.
> Phy filthy lecher lewde,
> Phy false unto thy wife,
> Phy coward phy . . .

And so on for seventeen more lines of *fies*. See George Gascoigne, *The Complete Works*, ed. John W. Cunliffe (Cambridge: Cambridge University Press, 1910; rpt. George Olms, 1974), II, 175-207. The lines are unnumbered. The above passage appears on p. 200.

[7]

what").[12] Among other more minor changes, for example, the writer of the *Ovide* has Progne sacrifice to the underworld god Pluto, a scene which is to be very important for him in the moralization. There is no need to linger over the tale itself, since the basic elements remain the same, but the moralization, which is so extravagant—and indeed, to modern ears certainly, absurd and contradictory of the main thread of the narrative—deserves quotation *in extenso*:

Now I will tell you the allegorical meaning of this fable. The king of the city of Athens is God, immortal King, all-powerful and eternal King, generous, kind, and merciful. His elder daughter Progne is the Soul, created by God in his own image and likeness, which he joined in marriage to the Body [Tereus], which he had formed of clay. The barbarians who waged war on the king of Athens were the Sons of Wickedness, Devils, who made war against God, thinking to take heaven from him. They, therefore, lost their realms and fell into the abyss of Hell, that horrible cage. It was for this reason that God brought about the marriage of Soul and Body, so that through them he could replenish Heaven, which had been emptied of the arrogant angels. It seems that the Body and Soul lived a long and happy life together. They brought forth a Son, that is, the Good Fruit of Holy Life [Itys]. And they had no wish to do evil but lived honorably in joyous and holy peace, until Progne, Human Nature, stooped to a most unseemly deed. She desired to see her sister, and decided to send the Body to bring her back. Philomena signifies Unsatisfying and Impermanent Love, that is, the Transitory Goods of this World. And God, in whom all goodness abounds, made these goods in order to sustain the human creature in moderation. Thus God caused Worldly Goods to appear in order to sustain man and woman, so that they would honor, serve, and adore him through these things. But in order to have these Vain Delights [i.e., Philomena], the Soul made

12. Ed. C. de Boer (Wiesbaden: Dr. Martin Sandig OHG, 1920; rpt. 1966), II, 366, lines 3685-86. Since the author of the *Ovide moralisé* mentions *Chrestiens* and since Chretien de Troyes himself remarks in the introduction to *Cligès* that he had written "de la hupe et de l'aronde et del rossignol la muance" (6-7), de Boer also had earlier (1909) edited the poem proper, without the moralization under the title *Chretien de Troyes, Philomena Conte Raconté d'Après Ovide*, with a lengthy introduction "proving" Chretien as the author. The ascription still remains a matter of debate. Indeed, however, any medieval poem on the subject was likely to be ascribed to Chretien de Troyes: on the folio preceding the *Rossignol* herein edited may be found the inscription "The 'Rossignol' is probably by Chrestien de Troyes," a chronological impossibility.

the Body cross land and sea. Yet she [Progne] sought nothing other than that which God had freely given, as long as it was used moderately. But the Body, in great excess, put all his thought and care in these things, and sought by force and violence to use them excessively, living a loose and dissolute life. He, therefore, imprisons her [Philomena] in a stronghold within a stone tower, since he wishes to live there, indulging his pleasure with Worldly Delight [i.e., Philomena]. An old woman, that is, Avarice, keeps her confined in the prison so that she cannot get away.

Meanwhile, the Soul [Progne] makes sacrifices and pays homage to Pluto in behalf of Worldly Delight [Philomena]. Sad and filled with fury, she strips off her golden dress and decks herself in black clothing. The golden dress signifies the ornaments of the holy and virtuous life, and the black and melancholy clothing denotes the sinful life, which the saddened and dishonored Soul dons because the Body betrays and abuses her with Vain Delight. Thus she makes offerings and sacrifice to Pluto and binds herself to him in behalf of Worldly Delight—and thereby forgets God her Creator, to whom all her desire should be directed. Thus does the Soul go beyond all the bounds of Reason; this is when Progne breaks down the prison which holds Philomena captive. Then when Wordly Delight emerges from the bonds of Covetousness, the Soul indulges herself in excess, wallowing in frenzied pleasure, as if mad and unbridled. She does nothing less than destroy her Spiritual Fruit [i.e., Itys] in order to feed and delight the greedy Body. And therefore through her uncontrolled passion, she destroys the Good Fruit of her life. And the sated body, because of its greedy belly, goes astray and turns to evil, shame, and corruption, thereby bringing the Soul to perdition in the chimney of Hell.

Therefore, it is clear that shortlived are the joys and quickly ended the delights of the one who seeks only to live in pleasure, pursuing merely the gratification of his disgraced and stinking flesh. For Pleasure invariably escapes him faster than the nightingale can fly. And the wicked, foolish Soul is lodged in the fire of Hell as soon as she flies away from him [i.e., the Body]. Thus the fable points to the truth. The stinking body becomes a hoopoe, filled with corruption, filth, and disgusting decay; and Vain, Changeable Delight becomes a flighty nightingale.

You have now heard the tale, as Chretien tells it, of the great crime committed by Tereus in the woods when he ravished his sister-in-law; how Progne became criminal and, to avenge Philomena, served the son to his father at table. On these people—unless the story lies—the gods took their revenge by turning all three into fickle birds for their great crimes.

[3687-3852]

[9]

Here, surely, is one of the saddest things that happens to the nightingale tradition—with every element of the poignantly tragic tale requiring reinterpretation along narrowly moralistic lines. No longer is there a *querens* philomena ceaselessly lamenting her ancient wrong. Instead, she has been glossed completely out of existence and has become a bloodless, no longer suffering creature, who is, of course, not even a creature but an idea, which like a mirror has deflected the suffering and tragedy from itself onto human existence. Thus Philomena signifies unsatisfying and impermanent human love (*amour decevable et faillie*, l. 3756), which is in turn simply a larger image of the vanity of all things terrestrial. Yet one must nevertheless not underestimate the rich possibilities of such a symbolic treatment. Under a delicate hand, it could have been a deeply tragic theme—as it is indeed to become with Peacham. In this particular context, however, didacticism rules absolutely, and thus the harsh warning, in Augustinian terms, against enjoying avidly, rather than merely using the transitory fruits of this life, for which sin, the reader is sternly admonished, one ends finally in the *infernal cheminee*.

John Gower too, in Middle English, recounts the story as a kind of exemplum within a larger context to illustrate a moral point, in this case the evil of *ravine* or rape. Although he does not, like the *Ovide moralisé*, attempt to equate every detail on a one-to-one allegorical level, his *moralité* nevertheless frequently leads him into trivial absurdities, even within what should have been his most pathetic and touching scenes. In the following scene, for example, where Philomene has just been released from prison and the two sisters are at last reunited, Progne sends up a prayer to Cupid and Venus, in which—with every hint of horror and tragedy missing—she is absurdly made to sound like nothing so much as a middle-class housewife who has somehow just discovered that her husband has been unfaithful to her:

> O ye, to whom nothing asterte
> Of love mai, for every herte
> Ye knowe, as ye that ben above
> The god and the goddesse of love;

Ye witen wel that evere yit
With al mi will and al my wit,
Sith ferst ye schopen me to wedde,
That I lay with mi lord abedde,
I have be trewe in mi degre,
And evere thoghte forto be,
And nevere love in other place,
Bot al only the king of Trace,
Which is mi lord and I his wif.
Bot nou allas this wofull strif!
That I him thus ayeinward finde
The most untrewe and most unkinde
That evere in ladi armes lay.
And wel I wot that he ne may
Amende his wrong, it is so gret;
For he to lytel of me let,
Whan he myn oughne Soster tok,
And me that am his wif forsok.[13]

Yet it is in the end of his narrative that Gower shows so clearly what is happening to the ancient story under the influence of new traditions. After recounting in detail all of the old Ovidian horrors—how Tereus, "that tirant raviner" [5627] had seized Philomene "riht as a wolf which takth his preie" [5633], or as "a goshauk hadde sesed a brid" [5644-5], and how after the deed "out he clippeth also faste hire tunge with a peire scheres" [5690-1]—after all this he describes how Philomene, as bird, "makth gret joie and merthe among" [5984], or more precisely he shows how her song is made up of mingled joy and woe, and goes on to explain it all away under the medieval topos of love as woeful joy:

Sche makth hir pleignte and seith, "O why,
O why ne were I yit a maide?"
For so these olde wise saide,
Which understoden what sche mente,

13. *Confessio Amantis*, V.5821-42. *The English Works of John Gower*, ed. G. C. Macaulay, EETS es 82 (London: Oxford University Press, 1901; rpt. 1957). Earlier, just before description of the rape, the narrator absurdly remarks that Tereus "Foryat he was a wedded man" (5631).

[11]

Hire notes ben of such entente.
And ek thei seide hou in hir song
Sche makth gret joie and merthe among,
And seith, "Ha, nou I am a brid,
Ha, nou mi face mai ben hid:
Thogh I have lost mi Maidenhede,
Schal noman se my chekes rede."
Thus medleth sche with joie wo
And with hir sorwe merthe also,
So that of loves maladie
Sche makth diverse melodie,
And seith love is a wofull blisse,
A wisdom which can noman wisse,
A lusti fievere, a wounde softe:
This note sche reherceth ofte
To hem whiche understonde hir tale.[14]

[5978-97]

And so, pathetically, has the antique, sweetly poignant story descended to the level of bathos, becoming merely an exemplum illustrating a mundane moral point and even a tediously pedantic disquisition explaining a literary convention. Gower's ending is clearly an awkward, heavy-handed attempt to reconcile the ancient sorrow with the new, powerful tradition of joyousness. But that melding of the two traditions had already been accomplished, a century earlier, by a far more powerful hand than the moral Gower's.

Nightingale as Poet

A minor but important theme in Antiquity is that of the nightingale as a metaphor for a human singer or poet. Hesiod, for example, recounts the story of a nightingale seized and threatened by a hawk, the poetic resonance of which suggests that the nightingale is to be equated with the poet himself threatened by a hawk-tyrant. Surely, Hesoid's refer-

14. Chandler [p. 79] speaks, oddly, of Gower's having "supplemented the Ovidian story with a beautiful passage on the nightingale and the meaning of her song."

ence to the understanding of the barons suggests a secondary level of meaning:

> Now I will tell you a fable for the barons;
>   they understand it.
> This is what the hawk said when he had caught
>   a nightingale
> with spangled neck in his claws and carried her
>   high among the clouds.
> She, spitted on the clawhooks, was wailing pitifully,
> but the hawk, in his masterful manner,
>   gave her an answer:
> "What is the matter with you? Why scream?
>   Your master has you.
> You shall go wherever I take you,
>   for all your singing.
> If I like, I can let you go. If I like,
>   I can eat you for dinner.
> He is a fool who tries to match his strength
>   with the stronger.
> He will lose his battle, and with the shame
>   will be hurt also."
> So spoke the hawk, the bird who flies so fast
>   on his long wings.[15]

Similarly, Euripides achieved the felicitous epithet of "honey-throated nightingale" of the stage,[16] and Pliny tells of the famous Sicilian Greek poet Stesichorus (fl. 632-552 B.C.), whose later fame was forecast from the cradle when a nightingale perched on his lips and sang.[17] In a slightly different turn to the image, Callimachus uses the image of the nightingale for poetry itself, impervious to death, in his elegy for his poet friend Heraclitus.[18] The evidence, thus, indicates a clear connection between poet and nightingale in Antiquity.

---

15. Works and Days, 202-12. *Hesiod*, trans. Richmond Lattimore (Ann Arbor: University of Michigan Press, 1968), p. 43.
16. Anth. Pal. VII.44. See also Pauly-Wissowa under *Luscinia*.
17. *Natural History* X.xliii.79-81.
18. Epigram II. For further examples see Pauly-Wissowa under *Luscinia*.

[13]

Although it is difficult to be precise about such matters, the
early use of this theme in Christian poetry argues a direct
line from Classical Antiquity. At all events, in this realm the
nightingale-poet is, as one might expect, the singer of divine
hymns to the Creator and Savior of the world. In the famous
ver avibus voces aperit, one of numerous poems to his patron
saint Felix, Paulinus of Nola (d. 431), for example, asks to be
given the spirit of the nightingale—

> . . . et uelut illam
> me modo ueris auem dulci fac uoce canorum
>
> Just as spring [gives voices to the birds], make me
> melodious like that bird with the sweet voice

and later,

> et tamen illius mihi deprecor alitis instar donetur[19]
>
> and, therefore, I beseech, let the image of that bird
> be given to me

—so that with a varied melody he may be able to sing the won-
ders of the Lord, as they have been manifested in St. Felix.

Similarly, Alcuin (d. 804) in his beautiful *De Luscinia*,
where the nightingale continually sings the praises of God:

> Spreta colore tamen fueras non spreta canendo,
>   Lata sub angusto gutture vox sonuit,
> Dulce melos iterans vario modulamine Musae,
>   Atque creatorem semper in ore canens.
> Noctibus in furvis nusquam cessavit ab odis
>   Vox veneranda sacris, o decus atque decor.
> Quid mirum, cherubim, seraphim si voce tonantem
>   Perpetua laudent, dum tua sic potuit?[20]

[7-14]

19. Ed. W. von Hartel, in *Corpus scriptorum ecclesiasticorum latinorum*, 30, 194-
206. Paulinus does not quite ask, as Wilhelm says, to be "transformed into a
nightingale." See J. J. Wilhelm, *The Cruelest Month* (New Haven: Yale Uni-
versity Press, 1965), p. 75.

20. An easily accessible text is in Philip Schuyler Allen, *The Romanesque
Lyric* (Chapel Hill: University of North Carolina Press, 1928; rpt. Barnes &
Noble, 1969), pp. 338-39; with translation on pp. 148-49. Curiously, Helen
Waddell (*Med. Latin Lyrics*) gives the poem, but breaks off before the end
without any indication of ellipsis.

Despised in color, though not in song, your broad voice sounded forth from your narrow throat, sending forth a sweet song in the Muse's varied melody, singing always the Creator of the world. Even in the darkest nights, that holy voice never ceased its divine odes, O splendor and beauty! What wonder if the Cherubim and Seraphim perpetually praise the great Thunderer, when you were able to sing in such a way?

If it is true (and there seems little doubt of it) that Alcuin masks a real person here under his private symbolism of the nightingale, the divine singing may, as usually interpreted, be simply a reference to the regular singing of the Church Offices.[21] Yet the feel of the poem suggests something more: note especially the Muse of line nine and the stress on the divine ability in lines thirteen and fourteen. Nor does it seem likely that the idea of the nightingale teaching its fellows how to enliven minds dead in sleep and wine (*ut nos instrueres vino somnoque sepultos*, l. 21) is merely a reference to a singing of the Hours. It may indeed be that the reference is to the religious poetry for which Alcuin and his school were famous.[22]

Yet whatever the case may be with Alcuin, the tradition of nightingale as poet was not, it would appear, ever a widespread or generally accepted one in the Middle Ages, not even in the later period when the metaphor becomes more direct and less ambiguous. There is no better evidence of this than the Introduction by an anonymous writer, clearly not the author himself, to John of Howden's Anglo-Norman *Rossignol*, a free translation-paraphrase by John himself of his Latin *Philomena*.[23] This introduction is an elaborate, almost

21. See Wilhelm, p. 91; also Eleanor S. Duckett, *Alcuin, Friend of Charlemagne* (New York: Macmillan, 1951), pp. 153-54, 297-98; and Waddell, *Med. Latin Lyrics.*, p. 305.

22. See Duckett, pp. 83-117.

23. A partial edition of Howden's *Rossignol* is available in Louise W. Stone, "Jean de Howden, Poète Anglo-Normand du XIIIe siècle," *Romania*, 69 (1946-7), 497-519; and his *Philomena* has been edited by Clemens Blume (Leipzig: O. R. Reisland, 1930). Since both Howden and Peacham wrote a *Philomena* and since both poems were translated into French, it is important to distinguish carefully between the two. Herein Howden's poem is entitled simply *Philomena*; Peacham's *Philomena praevia*.

desperate, attempt to explain the apparently enigmatic title of the poem:

> Ci comence la pensee Johan de Houedene, clerc la roine d'Engleterre, mere le roi Edward, de la neissance et de la mort et du relievement et de l'ascencion Jhesu Crist et de l'assumpcion Nostre Dame. Et a non ceste pensee: *Rossignos*, pur ce ke si come li rossignos feit de diverses notes une melodie, auci feit ceste livres de diverses matires une acordaunce. Et pur ce enkores a il non: *Rossignos*, que il estoit fez et trové en un beau verger flori ou rossignol adès chauntoient. Et pur ce fu il faiz que li quor celi qui le lira soit esprys en l'amour Nostre Seignour. Benoit soit qui le lyra. Ceste oevre comence. *Ci comence li Rossignol.*[24]

> Here begins the poem of John of Howden, clerk of the Queen of England, mother of King Edward, about the Birth, the Death, the Resurrection, and the Ascension of Jesus Christ, and of the Assumption of Our Lady. And this poem has the name of *Rossignol* because just as the rossignol makes a single melody out of various notes, so this work brings various matters into agreement. And it also has the name *Rossignol* because it was composed and made in a beautiful garden of flowers, where nightingales were then singing. And it was made for this reason: that whosoever shall read it may be illumined in the love of Our Lord. Blessed be the one who reads it. This work begins: *Here begins the Rossignol.*

The anonymous writer of this Introduction has clearly put forth his best efforts to explain; yet all of his various attempts smack of a kind of after-the-fact effort to understand a very awkward problem: why give the title *Rossignol* to a poem which has little or nothing to do with the rossignol? The writer has, however, read the poem thoroughly and well and is quite correct about its contents. The subject matter is indeed, as he makes clear, the Birth, Death, Resurrection, and Ascension of Christ, and the Assumption of the Holy Virgin—though he might have laid greater stress on the Passion, which is the poem's major concern.[25] And, as will be

---

24. See Stone, p. 501. The form *Rossignol* represents a normal Romance development from Latin *lusciniola*, diminutive of *luscinia*.

25. Stone [p. 503] writes: "Chaque épisode de la vie du Christ est ainsi motif à des réflexions pieuses, mais le poète passe en somme assez rapidement sur les événements de l'enfance; c'est pour la Passion de Jesus qu' il réservera toute son éloquence."

made clear in the appropriate section below, by the late thirteenth century this theme had become the peculiar property, as it were, of the nightingale. The fullest and most elaborate treatment of this theme is John Peacham's *Philomena praevia*, wherein *pia mens* (*devote âme* in the French) is merged absolutely with Philomena (Rossignol) and, alternately joyful and most wretched, sings the whole range of Christian history embodied in the Church Hours, from the Creation of man to the Incarnation and Crucifixion of Christ, but most especially the Passion. Thus, ironically from the standpoint of the explanatory Introduction, Howden's *Philomena* or *Rossignol* furnishes the clearest possible proof of the metaphorical oneness of poet and nightingale. Howden entitled his poem *Philomena* and *Rossignol*, because it is he himself in the guise of that tragic, joyous bird, who sings the Incarnation and Passion of Christ.

Finally, there is one slight, albeit highly ambiguous piece of evidence which may suggest that the nightingale, in its role as singer of worldly, licentious *amor*, was used as a term for a secular love poet. Alexander Neckam, for example, recounts the following bare, undetailed story of the nightingale:

> Sed o dedecus! quid meruit nobilis volucrum praecentrix, instar Hippolyti Thesidae, equis diripi? Miles enim quidam nimis zelotes philomenam quatuor equis distrahi praecepit, eo quod secundum ipsius assertionem animum uxoris suae nimis demulcens, eam ad illiciti amoris compulisset illecebras.[26]

> But O what a scandal! Why did that noble singer among birds, the very image of the chaste Hippolytus, deserve to be torn apart by horses? For a certain knight, who was filled with excessive jealousy, ordered the nightingale to be drawn and quartered by four horses, because, as he asserted, she so softened the spirit of his wife that she compelled her to illicit love.

In the preceding paragraph Neckam has just finished treating the nightingale on the metaphorical level as a religious contemplative,[27] and though this passage certainly is a swift,

---

26. *De naturis rerum*, ed. Thomas Wright, Rolls Series 34 (London: Longman, Green, 1863), 102-03.

27. See below, pp. 26-27.

illogical, and unexpected leap from one realm to another—
it is so in any case—to see his reference as a metaphor for a
secular love poet would relieve it of the absurdities conjured
up by nightingale *qua* nightingale being drawn and quartered
by horses. In any case, Neckam does not feel called upon to
elaborate: the tale (or event?) was apparently well known to
his audience, and for proof of this we have the outside evi-
dence of the Middle English *Owl and Nightingale* (late 13th
century?), which also alludes to the story in a similar context
of lascivous singing.[28]

Bird of Violence

Tempus, autem, quo solent reges ad bella procedere appelatur
Maius, quia tunc est tempus tranquillum et iocundum et temperatum,
in quo filomena cantum suum frequentat et herba abundanter invenitur
pro bobus et equis.[29] "That time is called May when kings are
accustomed to go out to war, because the weather is then
serene, happy, and temperate, a time when the nightingale
repeats her song and grass abounds for oxen and horses."
Thus writes Salimbene de Adam in a passage that, at first
sight, strikes one as extremely odd. Why should this Fran-
ciscan friar, in such a seemingly incongruous way, bring the
note of the nightingale into a context of war and prepara-
tion for war, to which this entire chapter of his work is given
over? One could, of course, argue that the passage is simply
ironic, even pacifistic, with its juxtaposition of the tranquil
happy season of nightingale song to the season of the clamor
of battle. Yet that does not seem to be the case. Rather, the
very syntax of the sentence, wholly divorced for the moment
from semantic considerations, demands a logical connection
between the clause containing the nightingale and the two

28. For the whole episode, see ll. 1049-1101. *The Owl and the Nightingale*,
ed. J. W. H. Atkins (Cambridge: Cambridge University Press, 1922), pp. 89-
93, and pp. 169-70 for translation into modern English. A more recent edi-
tion, without translation, by Eric G. Stanley is available in the Nelson Medi-
eval Library series (London: Thomas Nelson & Sons, 1960).

29. Salimbene de Adam, *Cronica*, ed. Giuseppe Scalia (Bari: G. Laterza,
1966), I, 569.

clauses that respectively precede and follow it. The clause *in quo filomena cantum suum frequentat* is sandwiched grammatically between *quo solent reges ad bella procedere* and *herba abundanter invenitur pro bobus et equis*, both of which have to do with war, and it is, moreover logically joined to the final clause by the coordinate conjunction *et*. All this, in terms of pure abstract syntax, requires a close grammatical connection among these varied segments of the sentence, and therefore in terms of meaning, a close connection between the song and war. The "kings prepare for war at that season *when* the nightingale reiterates her song *and when* grass abounds for (war) oxen and horses."[30] Without that last clause, the semantic link would be almost totally lost: the writer might well have aimlessly moved from thoughts of spring to the nightingale. With it, the logical connection seems inevitable —unless, of course, one were to argue that the writer himself was simply sloppy and aimless, and Salimbene was seldom that. In fact, the choice of the verb *frequentat* rather than, say, *cantat*, supports the foregoing analysis. The repeated cry of the bird is *oci, oci, oci*—or perhaps in Italian *occidi*[31]—the imperative of the Old French verb *occir*, and the call, therefore, is "kill, kill, kill."

A passage in the French romance *Jourdains de Blaivies* parallels Salimbene's usage exactly, since although again the cry of the bird is not given, the context makes quite clear the warlike associations that the nightingale holds for the poet. The romance, however, is far less oblique in its treatment, and the symbolic meaning of the bird could scarcely be overlooked:

30. The idea of kings going out to war in May is a medieval commonplace. Cf. the following from Bartholomaeus Anglicus (13th cent.) with Salimbene's Latin text: "Est autem Maius tempus amoenitatis, amotis & iucunditatis. Tunc enim maxime vociferant & gaudent aues. Tunc ad bella procedunt reges . . ." See *De rerum proprietatibus* (1601; rpt. Frankfurt/Main: Minerva, 1964), IX.xii.448.

31. Or *uccidi*. In any case, I have not found the cry of the bird so rendered in Italian, and when Jacomo da Porto translated *Philomena praevia* into Italian in 1585, he rendered the cry as *ochii*, without, apparently, recognizing any meaning in the word. See R. Köhler " 'oci, oci' als Nachtigallensang," *Zeitschrift für Romanische Philologie*, 8 (1884), 120-22.

En un vergier s'en entra maintenant,
Dou rousseingnol i a oi le chant,
Cil autre oisel se vont esbanoiant.
Lors li ramembre de Fromont le tyrant,
Qu'occist son pere a l'espee tranchant . . .[32]

Now he entered into a garden, where he heard the song of the
nightingale; all the other birds were making joy. Then he re-
membered Fromont the tyrant, who killed his father with a
trenchant sword.

This view of the bird as a reminder of or inciter to violence,
rather than passive victim, is, of course, a purely medieval
development, since it depends on word-play in the cry of the
bird not available to the Classical poet. The cry *oci, oci* as the
violent "kill, kill" is suggested in the *Roman de dame Aye*:

Et chantent li oisel et mainent grant delit
Et li roussignolet qui dit: Oci, oci!
Pucelle est en effroi qui loing set son ami.[33]

All the birds make great joy, along with the nightingale which
calls: Oci, oci! And the maiden who knows her lover to be far
away is frightened by it.

It is made fully overt in a highly comic passage of the
roman d'aventure *Wistasse le Moine*. The rascally hero
Eustace has stolen the Count of Boulogne's horses and has
led him on a wildly hilarious chase, resorting to various dis-
guises—now a potter, now a charcoal burner—along the way.
Finally, he climbs to the top of a tree:

En .j. nit d'escoufle est montés.
Wistasces li escervelés
Illuecques se fist loussignol.
Bien tenoit le conte por fol.
Quant voit le conte trespasser,
Wistasces commenche a criër:

---

32. As cited by Otto Glauning, ed. *Lydgate's Minor Poems: The Two Night-
ingale Poems*, EETS es 80 (London: Kegan Paul, 1900), p. 37. See the entire sec-
tion, pp. 35-38, for a discussion of the cry *oci*.

33. As cited by Glauning, p. 36.

"Ochi! ochi! ochi! ochi!"
Et li quens Renaus respondi:
"Je l'ocirai, par saint Richier!
Se je le puis as mains ballier."[34]

[1140-49]

Eustace the rascal climbed up into a kite's nest, and there he
pretended to be a nightingale. He held the count nothing but a
fool. When he sees the count passing by, he begins to cry out:
"Ochi! ochi! ochi! ochi!" And the count answers: "I will kill him,
by St. Richier, if I can get my hands on him."

Here then is the usual cry—*ochi* or *oci*—assigned the nightin-
gale in its violent role, of the many that it assumes in the
Middle Ages, and the meaning of the cry is brought fully and
openly to the surface in the comic translation provided by the
Count. The passage, however, continues at some length and
the poet has ingeniously worked in the varied trills and
roulades for which the song of the bird was famous in An-
tiquity, always with an appropriate French meaning, and
always with the *fols quens* acting as interpreter:

"Fier! fier!" dist Wistasces li moigne.
"Par foi!" dist li quens de Bouloigne,
"Si ferai jou, je le ferai,
Ja en cel liu ne le tenrai."
Wistasces rest aseürés,
Si se rest .ij. mos escriës:
"Non l'ot! si ot! non l'ot! si ot."
Quant li quens de Bouloigne l'ot,
"Certes si ot," che dist li quens;
"Tolu m'a tous mes chevals buens."
Wistasces s'escria: "Hui! hui!"
"Tu dis bien," dist li quens; "c'ert hui
Que je l'ocirai a mes mains.
Se je le puis tenir as mains."
Dist li quens: "Il n'est mie fol
Ki croit conseil de loussignol.

34. Ed. Wendelin Foerster and Johann Trost (1891; rpt. Geneva: Slatkine
Reprints, 1976).

Li loussignos m'a bien apris
A vengier de mes anemis,
Car li loussignos si m'escrie
Que je le fiere et que l'ochie."
Dont s'esmut li quens de Bouloigne
Por sievir Wistasce le moigne.

[1150-71]

"Fier! fier!" said Eustace the monk. "By my faith!" said the Count
of Boulogne, "I will strike him, I will strike him, but I cannot
find him here." Thus Eustace feels quite secure, and he cries out
two more words: *"Non l'ot! si ot! non l'ot! si ot!"* Hearing this, the
Count of Boulogne says: "Certainly he had him," said the
Count; "he has taken all my good horses." Eustace cried out:
"Hui! hui!" "You're speaking the truth, said the Count; "it will
be today that I kill him with my hands." Then the Count said:
"He is no fool who believes the advice of a nightingale. The
nightingale has taught me very well to take vengeance on my
enemy. For the nightingale cries out to me to strike him down
and kill him." Then the Count of Boulogne moved on to follow
after Eustace the monk.

The range of this seemingly rather limited view of the
nightingale is, in fact, surprisingly wide and varied, from
purely militaristic contexts, to an expression of the fright of
the lady separated from her *ami*, to the high comedy of *Wis-
tasse le moine*. Nor was it neglected in the shorter medieval
love lyrics, where it cries out against all those who are the
enemies of *fin' amour*:

Et si orrons le roussignol chanter
    En l'ausnoi,
Qui dit: "Oci ceus qui n'ont le cuer gai,
Douce Marot, grief sont li mau d'amer."[35]

And we hear the nightingale singing
    in the alder tree,
And she sings: "Kill all those who do not
    have gay hearts; O sweet Marot, the pains
of love are sharp."

The late Middle English *The Cuckoo and the Nightingale* wit-
nesses how widespread was an understanding of the French

35. As cited by Glauning, p. 37.

[22]

cry *oci*. In this pleasing little debate poem the Cuckoo asks the Nightingale why she always cries out *ocy, ocy*, and the Nightingale responds:

> "A fole!" quod she, "wost thou not what it is?
> Whan that I say '*ocy! ocy!*' y-wis,
> Than mene I that I wolde, wonder fayn,
> That alle they were shamfully y-slayn
> That menen aught ayeines love amis.
>
> And also I wolde alle tho were dede
> That thenke not in love hir lyf to lede;
> For who that wol the god of love not serve,
> I dar wel say, is worthy for to sterve;
> And for that skil '*ocy! ocy!*' I grede."[36]

[126-35]

Finally, and in a most surprising development, this vehement bird, giving full vent to its violent cry of *oci, oci*, makes its appearance in the Passion sequence itself, as may be seen in the proper section below.

Singer of the Divine

In his famous poem on the nightingale, Alcuin speaks not of Philomena but of Luscinia. It is a noteworthy fact that although writing a relatively pure Latin under the influence of the Classical Latin poets, who avoided the name Luscinia in favor of the metrically more suitable Philomela, Alcuin nonetheless deliberately preferred the less common form Luscinia. And for good reason. Philomela was not only still tainted, as we have seen, by the ancient tragedy, but, more importantly, Luscinia had long since in the Latin prose tradition been imbued with symbolic qualities fully appropriate for its treatment by the poets as a singer of the Divine. For the Middle Ages, Luscinia is etymologically associated with *Lux*, and is treated therefore as the harbinger of light, the singer of the sun, and thus, in Christian contexts, of *verus sol*, the true sun, that is, Jesus Christ. Thus in the

---

36. Ed. W. W. Skeat in *Supplement to the Works of Geoffrey Chaucer* (London: Oxford University Press, 1897; rpt. 1963), VII, 352.

poem, Alcuin's Luscinia never ceases its odes even in the darkest nights (*noctibus in furvis*) to the Creator, to the Thunderer, to the Lord. It is significant to note too the joyousness of this bird (*felix o nimus*), which forever sings God's praises, for this motif becomes of the highest importance in both the religious and the secular realms.

In the fourth century St. Ambrose writes of the joyousness of the nightingale, which sings at the dawn of the day:

> Utinam saltem luscinia canat, quae dormientem de somno excitet! Ea enim avis signare solet diei surgentis exortum, et effusiorem diluculo deferre laetitiam.[37]

> O let the nightingale sing, who wakes the sleeping man from his slumber! For that bird is accustomed to mark the dawn of the day, pouring forth its effusive joy in the early morning.

Now, although there are clear echoes here of Ambrose's famous hymn wherein it is the cock that performs the symbolic function of awakening Christian souls to the coming of the Light, nothing in this description really makes a concrete connection between Luscinia and *Lux*. Yet when Isidore of Seville (d. 636) takes up the description—and he clearly seems to be echoing Ambrose—he transforms the bird into the generic light-singer, and sets it on the way to becoming the singer of the One True Light:

> Luscinia avis inde nomen sumpsit, quia cantu suo significare solet diei surgentis exortum, quasi lucinia.[38]

> The bird Luscinia took its name from the fact that by its song it is accustomed to mark the dawn of the day, as if it were the light-bringer.

On the great authority of Isidore, the false etymology[39] becomes a medieval commonplace.

Thus in a late twelfth- or early thirteenth-century prose bestiary, the Rossignol is described as follows:

---

37. PL XIV.223.

38. *Etymologies* XII.vii.37.

39. The etymology might, in fact, be correct, but it is more likely that Luscinia is to be derived from *luges-cinia* "mournful singer." See Pauly-Wissowa under *Luscinia*.

Phisiologes nos dist que il se tient volentiers en beax forès et en beaus gardins, et cante tote nuit; et contre le jor se renvoisit et chante plus haut. Et quant il voit le soleil levé, si s'efforce de chanter, et demaine si grant joie de li meisme et de son chant qui tant li plaist, que por I poi que il ne se déront tot en chantant.

Cis oisèles est example de la sainte âme qui en la nuit de ceste vie atent nostre Segnor le vrai soleil de justice. Et quant èle sent qu'il est venus en son cuer par grasse (*grâce*), si a grant joie; si qu'èle ne le puet de[l] tot dire, ne del tot taire. Ceste joie a à non jubilation, que bouce ne le puet dire ne del tot taire.[40]

Physiologus tells us that it keeps itself gladly in beautiful forests and gardens, and sings all night long. And toward daybreak, it rejoices and sings all the louder. And when it sees the sun rise, it puts its whole spirit into singing, and it has such great joy of the sun and of its song that it is a great wonder that it does not burst in its singing.

This bird is a type of the holy soul, who, in the night of this life, awaits Our Lord, the true sun of justice. And when she feels that He has come into her heart by grace, she has great joy: she cannot express all her joy, nor yet can she keep silence. This joy is called jubilation, which the mouth cannot express, nor yet keep quiet about.

A late (c. 1325) medieval poem entitled *Poème moralisé sur les Propriétés des Choses* continues the tradition and cites the conventional etymology precisely, even while, it is noteworthy, listing the bird under its later form of Rosseignol:

> Rosseignol [si] est un oisel,
> Qui est et gracieus et bel;
> En une guise est coulourée,
> A couleur trait com encendrée;
> *Lucinia* est apelée
> Autrement, quar par li monstrée
> E[s]t la clarté du jour, quant vient;
> *A luce* est dit, si com dient.
> Entre les gens mout petit vient:
> Petit de char son cors contient,

40. C. Cahier and A. Martin, *Mélanges d'Archéologie, d'histoire et de littérature* (Paris: Poussielgue-Rusand, 1851), II, 159.

De quantité est mout petit,
De chanter a grant apetit;
En plumes habonde et en dis.
Li bois par lui est rebaudis:
Il chante par jour et par nuit.
Li oïr chanter est deduit;
Son chant est plain de grant douceur,
Muert en chantant de grant ferveur.[41]

The nightingale is a bird that is graceful and beautiful; It is a single color, like cinders. It is also called *Lucinia*, because it announces the dawn of the day; its name thus comes from *luce*, they say. It comes very little among people. It is extremely small, but it has a great zest for singing; it abounds in feathers and in song. The woods are made joyful through it: it sings both night and day, a joy to hear. Its song is filled with great sweetness. It dies through singing with such great fervor.

On such pseudo-etymological grounds, then, the nightingale becomes the singer par excellence of the Divine, the cantor of *le vrai soleil*, the true sun, and eventually, by a merging of many traditions, the creature identified with that most wrenching and at the same time most glorious of all events in Christian history, the very Passion itself.

It is not to be thought, however, that the nightingale as divine singer is wholly restricted to the bird as Luscinia. In the twelfth century, for example, Alexander Neckam writes of Philomena as a figure of the contemplative man, who joyously pours forth divine praises:

"Dulcius in solitis cantat philomena rubetis."[42] Sic et affectuosius dulcedini contemplationis vir contemplativus vacat in locis consuetis fructuosarum meditationum studio deputatis. Et ut poeticis alludamus figmentis, muta fuit quamdiu memor extitit injuriarum Terei, sed postea in avem mutata avibus in melodiae dulci varietate praeponenda censetur. Unde Martialis:

et quae
Muta puella fuit, garrula fertur avis.[43]

41. Ed. G. Raynaud in *Romania*, 14 (1885), 480.
42. Maximianus, *Elegies* II.49.
43. Martial, *Epigrams* XIV.lxxv.

[26]

Sic sic a laudibus divinis obmutescit rancorem fraterni odii quis nutriens in corde, sed postmodum tranquillitati vitae contemplativae deditus, hilariter os in laudes divinas aperit. Quid quod noctes tota[s] ducit insomnes, dum delicioso garritui pervigil indulget? Nonne jam vitam claustralium prae oculis cordis constituis, noctes cum diebus in laudem divinam expendentium? Loca multo frigori obnoxia, dum amoris vacat illecebris, avicula ista reformidat, quae si interim aliquo casu visitat, modulationibus dulcissimis operam non impendit.[44]

"The nightingale sings more sweetly in her accustomed bushes." And in the same way the contemplative man has leisure time for the sweetness of contemplation more lovingly in those places set aside for the study of fruitful meditation. And if we may speak poetically, the bird was silent as long as she remained mindful of the wrongs of Tereus, but afterward when she was changed into a bird, she was considered to be superior to all other birds in the variety of her sweet melody. Hence Martial says:

> she who
> was mute as a girl became a garrulous bird.

Just so whoever nourishes the rancor of fraternal hatred in his heart grows silent in his praises to God, but after he has been given wholly over to the tranquillity of the contemplative life, he opens his mouth gladly in divine praises. What is the meaning of the fact that the bird goes through long nights sleepless, indulging itself in a vigil of delightful warbling? Is not this the very image of the life of the cloisters, of those who spend whole nights and days in divine praise? Because it holds itself aloof from illicit love, this bird shuns evil places of great cold, and if perchance she does at times visit such places, she does not send forth her song of sweet melody.[45]

This version is especially noteworthy, because not only is the name Philomena used but the writer clearly bears in mind the Ovidian story, which, when recalled by the moralists, usually required a pejorative meaning for Philomena.

---

44. *De naturis rerum*, ed. Thomas Wright, Rolls Series 34 (London: Longman, Green, 1863), p. 102.

45. Neckam goes on to say that there is a famous river in Wales, on the British shore of which the nightingale sings, but if it happens to cross over to the opposite shore, it ceases its song immediately—a story which says a good bit more about Neckam's feeling toward the Welsh than about the nightingale.

The nightingale as a figure of the contemplative life also becomes a favorite image for another English writer, Richard Rolle of Hampole (d. 1449). Describing the stages of the contemplative life, for example, Rolle writes in *The Form of Living*:

> Bot þe sawle þat es in þe thyrd degre es als byrnand fyre, and as þe nyghttyngale, þat lufes sang and melody and fayles [i.e., dies] for mykel lufe; swa þat þe saule es anely comforted in lovying [i.e., praising] and lufyng of God, and til þe dede com es syngand gastly til Jhesu . . .[46]

Rolle was probably influenced by both Howden and Peacham,[47] and he returns to the symbol of the nightingale again and again. "In principio enim conversionis mee, et propositi singularis," he writes,

> cogitavi me velle assimilari avicule, que pre amore languet amati sui, sed languendo eciam letatur adveniente sibi quod amat et letando canit, canendo eciam languet, sed in dulcedine et ardore. Fertur enim philomena tota nocte cantui et melo indulgere, ut ei placeat, cui copulatur. Quanto magis cum suauitate maxima canerem Christo meo Jhesu, qui est sponsus anime mee per totam uitam presentem que nox est respectu future claritatis, ut langueam, et languendo deficiam pre amore.[48]

> In the beginning of my conversion and of my seclusion from the world, I sought to be like that bird which languishes for the love of its beloved, but, languishing, it also rejoices, realizing that it loves, and, rejoicing, it sings; but, while singing, it also languishes, but languishes in sweetness and ardor. For it is said that Philomena spends the whole night in song and melody, that it may please its mate. How much more should I sing with great sweetness to my Christ Jesus, who is my spouse during the present life which is night in respect to future brightness, sing that I may languish and, languishing, die for love.

In the late thirteenth century the Italian chronicler Salimbene de Adam recounts a charming story of a certain Brother

---

46. *English Writings of Richard Rolle*, ed. Hope Emily Allen (Oxford: Clarendon Press, 1931; rpt. 1963), p. 106.

47. See Hope Emily Allen, *Writings Ascribed to Richard Rolle* (New York: D. C. Heath, 1927), pp. 419-20 and n. 3.

48. *The Incendium Amoris of Richard Rolle of Hampole*, ed. Margaret Deanesly (Manchester: Manchester University Press, 1915), p. 277.

Minor named Vita, who was so well versed in music and was able to sing so beautifully that the nightingale itself would cease in awe to listen to him, and then the two would sing in alternation:

Item si quando cantabat philomena sive lisignolus in rubo vel sepe, cedebat isti, si cantare volebat, et ascultabat eum diligenter nec movebatur de loco, et postmodum resumebat cantum suum, et sic alternatim cantando voces delectabiles et suaves resonabant ab eis.[49]

Also if he wished to sing while Philomena or the nightingale was singing in the bushes or hedges, the bird deferred to him and listened to him diligently without moving from the place. Afterward it resumed its own song. And so they lifted up their delightful, sweet voices, alternately, in song.

A hundred years later it is St. Francis, we are told, who sings *alternatim* with Philomena:

Cum ipso libenter stabant volatilia: eum suo cantu, gestu, et mode laetificabant, sicut patuit in philomena quae in saepe consistens, per totam diem alternatim cum beato Francisco cantante cantavit . . .[50]

Birds stayed with him gladly and gladdened him with their song, movements, and manner. This was made clear by Philomena, who, sitting in a hedge, sang throughout a whole day alternately with the blessed Francis.

Finally, in the Scottish dialect of William Dunbar, the nightingale as singer of Divine Love is placed in direct and rather startling opposition to the *merle* (blackbird) as advocate of earthly love. "The Merle and the Nychtingaill" is a debate poem, and the two birds have at one another, in good Scottish fashion, for some fifteen stanzas.[51] The Merle is assigned the continually repeated refrain "A lusty lyfe in luvis service bene" opposing and finally being bested by the nychtingaill's "All love is lost bot upone God allone." At last the

49. Scalia, I, 264-65.

50. Bartholomaeo de Pisa, *De conformitate beati Francisci ad vitam Domini Iesu*, in *Analecta Franciscana*, 5 (1912), 21.

51. *The Poems of William Dunbar*, ed. W. Mackay Mackenzie (London: Faber & Faber, 1932), pp. 134-37.

poem ends where one knew, from the beginning, it would end, with *caritas* triumphant. And the reader is left with the exhortation that men should "luve the luve that did for his lufe de."

The Bird of Spring, Joy, and Love

It is again in the Latin tradition that the nightingale as a bird of joy and love first makes its appearance. In addition to the view of the bird as Luscinia, the blissful harbinger of light, the nightingale as a bird of elaborate and prolonged spring song goes back at least to Pliny's Natural History, in a passage which carried great weight in the Middle Ages:

Luscinis diebus ac noctibus continuis xv garrulus sine intermissu cantus densante se frondium germine, non in novissimis digna miratu ave. primum tanta vox tam parvo in corpusculo, tam pertinax spiritus; deinde in una perfecta musicae scientia: modulatus editur sonus, et nunc continuo spiritu trahitur in longum, nunc variatur inflexo, nunc distinguitur conciso, copulatur intorto, promittitur revocato; infuscatur ex inopinato, interdum et secum ipse murmurat, plenus, gravis, acutus, creber, extentus, ubi visum est vibrans—summus, medius, imus. . . . ac ne quis dubitet artis esse, plures singulis sunt cantus, nec iidem omnibus, sed sui cuique. certant inter se, palamque animosa contentio est; victa morte finit saepe vitam, spiritu prius deficiente quam cantu.

Nightingales pour out a ceaseless gush of song for fifteen days and nights on end when the buds of the leaves are swelling— a bird not in the lowest rank remarkable. In the first place there is so loud a voice and so persistent a supply of breath in such a tiny little body; then there is the consummate knowledge of music in a single bird: the sound is given out with modulations, and now is drawn out into a long note with one continuous breath, now varied by managing the breath, now made staccato by checking it, or linked together by prolonging it, or carried on by holding it back; or it is suddenly lowered, and at times sinks into a mere murmur, loud, low, bass, treble, with trills, with long notes, modulated when this seems good—soprano, mezzo, baritone. . . . And that no one may doubt its being a matter of science, the birds have several songs each, and not all the same but every bird songs of its own. They compete with one another, and there is clearly an animated rivalry between them; the loser often ends her life by dying, her breath giving out before her song.[52]

There are a number of elements here that assume great importance for the medieval nightingale: the small body but powerful voice, the rivalry among the birds, the death of the bird through its strenuous efforts, and, of especial importance here, the wild cries of the bird poured forth in the springtime.

As early as the eleventh century, its joyous notes sound forth, among a chorus of others, in a lively reverdie:

> Vestiunt silve tenera merorem
> virgulta, suis onerata pomis;
> canunt de celsis sedibus palumbes
>   carmina cunctis.
>
> . . . .
>
> Hic leta canit philomela frondis,
> longas effundit sibilum per auras
> sollempne; milvus tremulaque voce
>   ethera pulsat.[53]

The shady groves are crowned with leafy branches, laden with fruit; sitting on high, doves send forth their many songs.
. . . .
Hidden among the leaves, Philomela sings and pours forth her long and stately airs; and the blackbird with her tremulous voice strikes the heavens with her song.

Yet, in point of fact, although striking the very accents of later spring/love songs, this poem does not actually embody the theme of the amorous bird of later tradition, as one is led to expect by the fully conventional opening. Unexpectedly, though in retrospect quite naturally, in its sixth and final stanza the poem very simply manifests itself, in an unassuming extension of its basic imagery of joyous birds exulting in the serene weather, as a religious hymn to the happy occasion of the Incarnation of Christ.

52. Both text and translation are those of H. Rackham, *Pliny, Natural History*, Loeb Classical Library (Cambridge, Mass.: Harvard University Press, 1967), III, 344-45.
53. Whicher, p. 18.

Nulla inter aves similis est api,
que talem tipum gerit castitatis
nisi que Christum baiulavit alvo
    inviolata.

Yet none of the birds is like to the bee, which is the very type of
chastity, excelled only by that one who, inviolate, bore the Christ
in her womb.[54]

The poem is finely crafted, adapting, in its carefully under-
stated manner, the conventional natural setting to the ex-
pression of deep religious feeling. After all the emphasis
upon the sweet new season throughout the poem, the reader
is suddenly brought up short and made aware in this final
stanza that the poet has been singing the glories of the Cre-
ator throughout, and then the proper readjustments come
automatically—to Lady Day in the springtime, to the annual
recreation of the world in the springtime, a universal figure
of the original creation which took place in the springtime,
and (if we can assume that spring and love were already
closely associated, and indeed we must) to the Love that
condescended to take on human flesh by housing itself in
alvo virginis.

But more closely related to the immediate theme in hand
is the twelfth-century *Clausus Chronus* with its bird of pure
earthly *amor* (and no other bird save the nightingale, it is
important to note, makes an appearance):

vernant veris ad amena
thyma, rose, lilia,
his alludit filomena,
melos et lascivia.[55]

Roses, thyme, lilies come again in the sweetness of the spring,
and Philomena, melodious and wanton, plays sportively.

54. There is a pun in this last line, since *alvus* ("womb") also means
"beehive." Because they were thought to bring forth virginally, bees were
frequently linked with the Holy Virgin in the Middle Ages. A miniature of an
Exultet Roll from Gaeta shows a Nativity with beehives and working bees.
See Francis Klingender, *Animals in Art and Thought* (Cambridge, Mass.: M.I.T.
Press, 1971), p. 249. Klingender, however, misinterprets the picture.

55. Whicher, p. 46.

A later stanza of this poem is also significant in its focus on the theme which is to become an unrelenting commonplace of the vernacular lyrics—the distance between man and nature, and the sorrow of the lover juxtaposed to the joy of the natural world:

> Si quis amans per amare
> amari posset mereri
> posset amor mihi velle mederi,
> quod facile sibi, tandem beare,
> perdo querelas absque levare.

If a wholehearted lover could deserve to be loved, Love might be willing to heal me, even bless me, which he could do easily, but, as it is, I waste my plaints fruitlessly.

Note the *querelas* of the last line; it is almost as if the complaints and sorrow of the Ovidian nightingale have been displaced from the bird and transferred to the lover.

Perhaps the best example of this Latin bird as the perfect exemplar of joy and love, however, is the lilting *Tempus est iucundum* of the *Carmina Burana*, where again only the nightingale is present:

> Tempus est iucundum,
> o virgines,
> modo congaudete,
> vos iuvenes.
> > O. o. totus floreo,
> > iam amore virginali
> > totus ardeo,
> > novus novus amor
> > est, quo pereo.
> > Cantat philomena
> > sic dulciter
> > et modulans auditur;
> > intus caleo.[56]

Splendid is the weather, O virgins! Have joy now together, all you young people.

56. *Ibid.*, p. 218.

[33]

O, O, I am all flowered forth; now I am all aflame with a virginal love; it is a new, new love that I am dying from. Philomena sings so sweetly, echoing melodiously; I am burning up, within.

The poet even has to call for the nightingale to cease in its love songs so that his own cantilena may rise from his heart:

> Sile, philomena,
> pro tempore,
> surge, cantilena,
> de pectore.

Keep still for a time, Philomena. Rise up, o my songs.

And the poem ends on the joy and the dying away for love, but the "death" here is a far cry from the complaining *querelas* of the preceding poem; it is rather a swooning away in the very throes of love, a theme which is to be transformed in the religious tradition into the mystical experience of divine *caritas*:

> veni, domicella,
> cum gaudio,
> veni, veni bella,
> iam pereo.

Come, lady, joyously! Come, come, beautiful one! Now, I am dying.

It is, however, in the vernacular poetry that Philomena—rather *rossignol, nahtegal, nightegale*—comes fully into her own as the supreme bird of love and the joyous new season. Note the total obsession with joy and love in the opening of Bernart de Ventadorn's beautiful *Can l'erba fresch' e lh folha par*:

> Can l'erba fresch' e·lh folha par
> e la flors boton' el verjan,
> e·l rossinhols autet e clar
> leva sa votz e mou so chan,
> joi ai de lui, e joi ai de la flor
> e joi de me e de midons major;
> daus totas partz sui de joi claus e sens,
> mas sel es jois que totz autres jois vens.

[1-8]

When the new grass and the leaves come forth
and the flower burgeons on the branch,
and the nightingale lifts its high
pure voice and begins its song,
I have joy in it, and joy in the flower,
and joy in myself, and in my lady most of all;
on every side I am enclosed and girded with joy,
and a joy that overwhelms all other joys.[57]

The nightingale becomes a true messenger of love for Peire d'Alvernhe (fl. 1150-80), who sends it as his love-servant to his lady—*Rossinhol, el seu repaire m'iras ma dona vezer*, "Nightingale, you will go for me to see my lady in her residence"— and, in a sequel poem, she sends it back again with the assurance of her love *de bon coratge*, "with her whole heart."[58]

---

57. Both text and translation are those of Frederick Goldin, *Lyrics of the Troubadours and Trouvères: An Anthology and a History* (Garden City: Anchor Books, 1973), pp. 136-39.

58. Ibid., pp. 162-69. The nightingale as a messenger of love becomes fully conventional. Compare the following:

> Rossignolet qui chante par dessoubz l'olivier,
> va t'en dire à m'amye que d'elle pres congé.

> Rossignolet who sings beneath the olive tree,
> Go and tell my beloved farewell for me.

And also:

> Rossignolet sauvaige, prince des amoureu(l)x!
> je te prie qu'il te plaise de bon cueur gracieulx,
> va moy faire ung messaige à la belle à la fleur,
> qu'elle ne m'y tienne plus [en] si grosse rigueur.

O wild Rossignolet, prince of lovers! Please go and take a message to the beautiful lady, and ask her not to treat me so haughtily any longer.

And in another the nightingale herself is presented as speaker:

> Roxignolet m'apele l'on,
> que héent li vilain félon;
> mès cil qui ont d'amer corage,
> font toz jors de moi lor message,
> quar je sui légiers et menuz.
> Entendez por qoi sui venuz;
> quant je bone novele aporte,
> bien me devez ouvrir la porte.

I am called Rossignolet. The wicked hate me, but true lovers always make me their messenger, because I am small and light. You should under-

This, as we shall see, is to become an important theme for Peacham.

Here then is the dominant tradition of the nightingale in the Middle Ages, the bird bursting with *joie*, pouring forth its sweet exhilarating love songs in the spring. In this area, it becomes the bird of *fin' amor, amor de lonh*, of simple human love between man and woman, of sensuous, even sensual, lascivious love; it is a symbol which soars to the highest, most idealistic and yet descends to the lowest, most licentious, even comic levels of terrestrial, worldly love. And it sings with many voices—in Latin—*O.o. totus floreo*—in Provençal, in English, German, French, and Italian. "When the nightegale singes," writes an English poet of the late thirteenth or early fourteenth century:

> The wodes waxen grene:
> Lef and gras and blosme springes,
> In Averil, I wene.
> And love is to mine herte gon
> With one spere so kene . . .[59]

And it is the sweet song of the nightingale that Walther von der Vogelweide employs for his quietly simple yet intricately complex symbol of a young girl's love, short-lived yet beautiful, or perhaps exquisitely beautiful *because* short-lived:

> Under der linden
> an der heide,
> da unser bette was,
> da muget ir vinden
> schone beide
> gebrochen bluomen unde gras.

stand why I have come: when I bring good news, you should open the door to me.
See Ludwig Uhland, *Schriften zur Geschichte der Dichtung und Sage* (Stuttgart: Cotta'iche Buchhandlung, 1865-73), III, 170-71.

59. *Medieval English Lyrics*, ed. R. T. Davies (Evanston: Northwestern University Press, 1964), p. 62.

> Vor dem walde in einem tal,
> tandaradei,
> schone sanc diu nahtegal.[60]

Under the linden on the heath, where we two had our bed together, there you can find both the flowers and the grass broken down. In a little valley before the wood, tandaradei, beautifully sang the nightingale.

This splendid little lyric would not, of course, have worked at all without a full, elaborate tradition implied by Vogelweide's *nahtegal*.

Examples from the lyrics could be multiplied almost indefinitely; the tradition becomes so fully conventional that the love poet can scarcely do without his nightingale.[61] Yet, as might be expected, some of the most notable developments occur in the longer, more leisurely, narrative structures. Surely, one of the finest, most symbolically suggestive of these—and to my mind perhaps the greatest short tale in medieval literature—is the *Lai de Laustic* of Marie de France.[62] What Marie manages to do in this lai is to take the nightingale, already a background symbol of idealistic love in lyric poetry, and body it forth in fully rounded form as a figure of the *summum bonum* of earthly love, delicately balanced, exquisite, and therefore sadly perishable—all the while preserving the luminous yet enigmatic quality of the symbol. And that is no mean accomplishment! Briefly, the story line is as follows:

There were two worthy knights of the realm of Brittany—one married, the other a bachelor—so well spoken of and admired by all that their city of St. Malo achieved great fame thereby. The bachelor knight gains the love of the other's wife; yet the two

60. *Die Gedichte Walthers von der Vogelweide*, ed. Carl von Kraus (Berlin, 1950), p. 62.

61. The nightingale as a bird of joy becomes almost fully proverbial in Middle English. See *Proverbs, Sentences and Proverbial Phrases From English Writings Mainly Before 1500*, ed. Bartlett Jere Whiting and Helen Wescott Whiting (Cambridge, Mass: Harvard University Press, 1968).

62. See the recent edition by Jeanne Lods, *Les Lais de Marie de France* (Paris: Librairie Honore Champion, 1959).

[37]

are so discreet that no one knows of their love. They had little to displease them save that they were unable to take their pleasure together as often as they desired. The lady was strictly guarded when her husband was away. Nevertheless, their castles are so close together that from their casements they are able to exchange fair looks and even to toss over missives and small presents. In the spring when the nightingale sings so beautifully, the lady becomes so enamored of the bird's song that she slips out to the casement in the dark and spends much of the night in vigil with her lover. She does this so frequently that her husband becomes angered and demands the reason of her absences. When she answers that it is because of her joy in the singing of the nightingale, her husband is filled with wrath and malice. He has his servants trap the bird and angrily brings it to his wife, wrings its neck, and tosses its limp body on her knees, in such a manner that her breast is sprinkled with its blood (*si que sun chainse ensanglanta/Un poi desur le piz devant*, ll. 118-19).[63] Sadly, she takes up the body, berating her fate. And she assumes from the moment of the bird's death that her love affair with her *ami* is at an end. "Never again will I be able to rise at night and go to the window, where I used to see my lover; of one thing I am sure: he will think that I am playing him false" (*Ne purrai mes la nuit lever,/N'aler a la fenestre ester,/ U suleie m'ami veer./Une chose sai jeo de veir:/Il quidera ke jeo me feigne* ll. 127-31). She sends the bird's body to her lover, who has it encased in a precious casket and carries it with him ever afterwards.

Thus with such splendid economy and artistic poise does Marie make use of and at the same time give new depth to the symbolic nightingale. Whatever it is that the husband has managed to do—and it is one of Marie's finest virtues that she absolutely refuses to become prosaic and literal—it is clear that he has been the "winner" in the love triangle; without ever even fully understanding, he has been able to destroy that fair, living, but all too fragile bond between the two lovers. It can thereafter be enshrined in gold and precious stones and preserved forever, but it is a memory that is preserved; the life has departed.

Despite traces of the fabliau in the *Lai de Laustic*, the nightingale and the love embodied by it remain on the highest

---

63. How strangely transformed but still Ovidian is the breast spattered with blood.

possible level; this is *fin' amor* at its most refined. It was left to Boccaccio (*Decameron*, v.4) to reduce the whole tradition to broad, farcical comedy. In the tale, the young girl Caterina persuades her parents to allow her to sleep on the balcony (where she will be accessible to her lover) by pleading the heat of her room and her desire to listen to the nightingale. Against her father's better instincts, she achieves her wish. Her lover comes, spends the night with her, and then unfortunately oversleeps and is discovered in *flagrante delicto* by the parents. During the course of the story, as T. A. Shippey has pointed out, the expressions *udendo cantare l'usignuolo, faccendo cantare l'usignuolo*, etc., become "comic periphrases for sexual intercourse," and when the father, who makes the discovery, calls out, "Get up at once, wife, and come and see how your daughter is so fond of the nightingale that she has caught it and is still holding it in her hand," the bird has become "finally identified with the male organ" itself.[64] The story ends happily: the young man is required to marry the girl, since he has put the nightingale in its proper "cage" (*gabbia*), but the bird, as a singer of high romantic love in Italian literature, can scarcely be said ever to have fully recovered.

The Passion

The *Gesta Romanorum* (thirteenth century) recounts a version[65] of the tale told by Marie de France in the *Lai de Laustic*; here, however, all of Marie's eloquent silences are disrupted, with every narrative element being brought flatly and simplemindedly to the surface: the lady is married to an old man; and her lover-knight, interestingly, is married too, to an old woman; the nightingale sings from its tree (a fig tree, we are told); when the malicious old husband kills the sweet-singing bird, the young knight is so incensed that he makes war on

---

64. "Listening to the Nightingale," p. 52. Cf. also the ballad called "The Bold Grenadier," picked up in a number of versions by Cecil J. Sharp in the early 1900s, printed in James Reeves, *The Idiom of the People* (Heineman, 1958), pp. 85-87.

65. Tale CXXI.

him and slays him; his own old wife then, happily, dying, the young knight weds the lady. One could scarce think of a more degraded mangling of Marie's story. Yet, as with the original author, the moralization is the important matter here. The two knights, we are told, are Moses and Christ. The young wife is the New Law who listens to the nightingale, that is, the Humanity of Christ, singing from the fig tree, that is, from the Cross. Now, it is true that in the surreal moralistic world of the *Gesta Romanorum* almost any event or detail in the mundane world may be transformed on the higher level into any other event or detail for the sake of the moral, without any very clear logical connection between the two. Frequently, of course, from our point of view, all logic is totally defied. Thus it is not surprising to find a story whose basic fabliau plot—"she strove mightily to win him to marriage, if possible, upon the death of her own old husband"[66]—deals with frank, illicit human love reinterpreted in terms of Christ, *caritas*, and the new law of the Church. Yet in this case the nightingale must have served as a powerful stimulus toward the particular interpretation adopted, because the bird had already become closely associated with the event of the Passion.

As early as the eleventh century in the curious beast epic *Ecbasis Captivi*, Filomena sings at great length of Christ's suffering during the Passion, and is almost overcome in her strenuous efforts and her vicarious suffering. In the scene both Filomena and the *merule* (blackbird) are brought before the lion, king of the beasts, to minister to him with song, and they sing a duet in order to lull him off to sleep:

> Concentu parili memoratur passio Christi.
> Passer uterque deum cesum flet verbere Iesum,
> Exanimis factus, claudens spiramina flatus;
> Commutat vocem, dum turbant tristia laudem,
> Organa divertit, dum Christi vulnera plangit,
> Solvitur in luctum recolens dominum crucifixum,

---

66. *Omnibus viribus nitebatur, si possibile esset, in virum accipere post mortem viri sui.* Hermann Oesterley, ed., *Gesta Romanorum* (Berlin: Weidmannsche Buchhandlung, 1872), p. 471.

Squalet se cinere, dum fertur mocio terre;
Offuscat visum, memorans solem tenebratum.
Hii gemini trepidas pressere ad pectora palmas,
Vnicus ut matre, sic deflent hii pacientem.
His avibus motis stupuit milicia regis . . .[67]

[838-48]

In smooth harmony the two birds sing the Passion of Christ.
They both lament the Lord Jesus wounded by the lash; becom-
ing almost lifeless in their emotion, they almost lose their power
of breath. But they change their voices, because sad things dis-
turb their praise; they sing in a new key when they lament the
wounds of Christ; they are almost dissolved in grief remem-
bering the Lord crucified; they sprinkle themselves with ashes
when they sing of the earthquake; their vision is darkened,
remembering the darkened sun. They press trembling hands to
their breasts. They weep over the Passion, just as the Mother
herself did for her only begotten Son. The followers of the king
wondered greatly at the great emotion of these birds.

Although the song itself is delivered in concert with the black-
bird, it becomes quite evident in the following scenes that
Filomena alone is, for the poet, preeminently the bird of the
Passion. After the song, for example, she continues to grieve
and must be comforted by the Panther:

Pardus: "Plurima sat passi tractasti vulnera Christi;
             Desine, cara, precor, iam desine fundere fletus,
             Nobiscum gaude, depellens tristia plaude."

Filomena: "Nunc precor, ut dicas, cur me gaudere
                rogabas.
             Vnde etenim tristi persuades parcere menti?
             Sunt mihi leta quidem, sed tanto pondere
                mentem
             Infero lugentem, quod me nec vivere vellem,
             Sepius exopto gelido me tradere leto."

[907-14]

---

67. Edited, translated by Edwin H. Zeydel (Chapel Hill: University of
North Carolina Press, 1964). The translation here is by the editors of this
work; Zeydel's is somewhat overly literal. In view of later traditions, it is
important to note that the nightingale here also sings of the Nativity.

[41]

Panther: "You have treated fully enough the wounds of the suffering Christ; now leave off, dear one, cease pouring forth your sighs. Have joy with us, rejoice, putting aside all sadness."

Filomena: "Now, I beseech, why do you ask me to rejoice; why do you persuade me to spare my sad mind? These things are indeed joys to me, but I bear such a grieving mind weighed down with so heavy a burden that I do not wish to live. Very often indeed I wish to be given over to cold death."

How strangely the varied strands of the old traditions have come together and intertwined here, with seemingly incongruous and mutually exclusive motifs becoming unexpectedly consonant with one another: Alcuin's joyful bird singing to the glorious Creator, the antique *querula* Philomela bewailing her ancient wrong, Pliny's strenuous bird pouring out its whole soul, sometimes even to death, in its straining efforts.

It is upon this foundation that John Peacham built in the late thirteenth century. And Peacham's masterful achievement in the *Philomena praevia* derives largely from the fact that he has perceived the basic strength of the assimilative and harmonizing process inherent within his inherited material and—without once descending into the absurdity usual to this brand of medieval overreaching—has extended the method far beyond what would appear to be its natural and reasonable boundaries. Thus almost every motif associated with the nightingale, almost every nuance of emotion, has been made an integral part of his design. A wild, violent bird shrieking out its cry of "Kill, kill, kill" in the context of a Passion poem? This is precisely what Peacham manages. Alternately weeping and rejoicing throughout each of the Hours of the day and reaching a crescendo at the Hour of the Crucifixion, his Philomena cries out in lamentation a thousand times *Oci, oci, oci miseram*[68] ("Kill, kill, kill wretched

68. Here and elsewhere in this Introduction, I have used the Latin text for purposes of discussion, since the French is very faithful to the original and is readily available herein. Because the stanza numbers correspond exactly, the French text may be easily consulted.

[42]

me"), a call which achieves its fruition finally at Nones, the Hour of Christ's final *Consummatum est* from the cross, when the bird achieves its longed-for death, the love/death of the mystical experience.

Even the very verse form Peacham chose calls to mind other, different traditions, for he employed the famous so-called "Goliardic" measure so fully redolent of *Philomena lascivia*.[69] The opening stanzas, in fact, could be paralleled closely by numerous examples—an almost endless supply, of course, in the vernaculars—from secular love poetry; there is simply no hint, save in retrospect, that this particular love is on a vastly higher plane:

> Philomena, praevia
> temporis amoeni,
> Quae recessum nuntias
> imbris atque caeni,
> Dum demulces animos
> tuo cantu leni,
> Avis prudentissima,
> ad me, quaeso, veni.
>
> Veni, veni, mittam te,
> quo non possum ire,
> Ut amicum valeas
> cantu delinire,
> Tollens eius taedia
> voce dulcis lyrae,
> Quem, heu, modo nequeo
> verbis convenire.

Philomena, harbinger of the sweet season, you who announce the return of the spring rain and loam, you who make spirits mild with your soft song, O wise bird, come, I ask, to me.

Come, come, I will send you to that one whom I cannot approach, so that with your song you may anoint a friend, taking his weariness away with the voice of your sweet lyre, that man whom, alas, I cannot speak to now.

69. See Raby, "Philomena praevia," pp. 444-45.

[43]

All the usual trappings of the medieval poetry of *fin' amor* are here: the conventional and expected *Natureingang*, the sweet new season, the bird as a *messager* of love, etc.

The wise bird of line seven may indeed strike an odd chord, but not enough to disturb the general harmony of the reverdie in this opening scene. It is only on the second time around, only in re-reading that one suddenly realizes that this is an *avis prudentissima* because it belongs to the tradition of Alcuin's Luscinia who joyously sings continual praises to the *Creatorem*, or that of the bestiary, where *cis oisèles* is an *example de la sainte âme qui en la nuit de ceste vie atent nostre Segnor le vrai soleil de justice*. During the course of his poem, Peacham works out in minute detail the correspondences between his Philomena and the *anima plena amore*, "soul filled with love" (stanza 12), who sings through each of the Hours and finally dies in languor and ecstasy at Nones.

It might even be argued, of course, that the structure of the poem is too tight and rigid, that the correspondences between bird and soul are made far too overtly and baldly explicit. And it is certainly not to be denied that the poem does at times become almost woodenly prosaic in its rigid insistence on higher meaning, much like certain medieval biblical glossing with its overabundance of *significat*'s. The point is clearly not meant to be missed:

> Restat, ut intellegas
>   esse philomenam
> Animam virtutibus
>   et amore plenam,
> Quae, dum mente cogitat
>   patriam amoenam,
> Satis favorabilem
>   texit cantilenam.
>
> [St. 12]

You should understand that Philomena is the soul filled with virtue and love, who composes a very beautiful song when she contemplates her delightful homeland.

There must be no mistake: Philomena *significat animam*. Moreover, the poet flatly informs us that the bird's last day of sing-

ing is God's gift to the soul of a *quaedam dies mystica* for the
augmentum . . . suae sanctae spei ("a certain mystical day for
the augmentation of its holy hope"); that the song at dawn
is the soul's joyous reliving of the creation; that the song at
Nones is (as Gower put it) a song of "joyful wo," through
which the nightingale/soul dies in mystical ecstasy, etc., etc.

Furthermore, it is certainly true that although concerned
with defining poetically a vaguely indefinable kind of reli-
gious passion, the poem at the same time deals in a wealth of
mundane detail and minutiae. Yet it is, of course, precisely
because the poem deals with the indefinable that it grounds
itself in hard fact, the hard "fact," for one, of Pliny's natural
history. When, for example, the nightingale *qua* nightingale
sings between midday and Nones, it very literally begins to
fall apart:

> Tunc disrumpit viscera
> nimio clamore
>
> . . . .
>
> Sic quassatis organis
>
> . . .
>
> Rostro tantum palpitans
> fit exsanguis paene,
> Sed ad nonam veniens
> moritur iam plene,
> Cum totius corporis
> Disrumpuntur venae.

[St. 9, 10]

Then its entrails burst with the effort of its cry. With its organs
shattered. With the throbbing of its throat, with all the veins of
its body burst asunder, death arrives at last at the Ninth Hour.

Here are the concrete, vivid natural "facts" of the real world;
in terms of the poem, of course, they are images too of a
real-er reality: all these objective facts

> Mystice conveniunt
> legi Iesu Christi.

[St. 11]

Conform mystically to the law of Jesus Christ.

[45]

There is no better example in the poem of this mingling of mystical experience with minute detail than in the scene where the nightingale/soul expresses its desire to have been at the Nativity and early childhood of Christ:

Heu me, cur non licuit
   mihi demulcere
Vagientem parvulum,
   dulciter tenere,
Illos artus teneros
   sinu refovere
Eiusque cunabulis
   semper assidere.

. . . .

O quam dulce balneum
   ei praeparassem,
O quam libens umeris
   aquam adportassem,
Praesto matri virgini
   semper ministrassem
Pauperisque parvuli
   pannulos lavassem.

[St. 30, 33]

Alas, why was I not allowed to caress the weeping child, to hold him gently, to warm his tender little limbs in my bosom, and to sit always beside his cradle. O what a sweet bath I would have prepared for him, O how gladly I would have carried the water on my shoulders; I would have always been near to minister to the Virgin mother, and I would have washed the swaddling clothes of the poor little boy.

Peacham's most notable achievement in this mystical poem, however, is his thorough merging of the two widely divergent traditions of joy and sorrow. For the poem depicts not only *philomena leta*, singing ecstatically at Matins the joys of the creation, but also *philomena querens* at Prime, weeping with the weeping child of the Nativity, and, at Meridiem, lamenting inconsolably at the sight of the Christ on the cross. Yet the merging is not simply a matter of bringing together the two motifs, alternating the one with the other within the bounds of a single poem; rather, it is an absolute fusion of

[46]

the two. For what finally emerges, in the mystical vision of the poet, is *gaudium in luctu*, joy in grief or, perhaps, joy as grief and grief as joy: *Gemitus, suspiria, lacrimae, lamenta*, the poet writes, *sibi sunt deliciae* ("Groans, sighs, tears, laments, these are its delights," St. 77). And, finally, in the tradition of Pliny—*spiritu prius deficiente quam canti*—or as Peacham says, *cum amoris impetus rumpit carnis frenum*, "when the rush of love breaks the rein of flesh," it dies, pierced by the spear of love, but *felici morte*, "with a happy death." And for such a one we do not sing a Requiem, but rather the Introit of the Mass—*Gaudeamus*, "let us rejoice."

Other Images

In a poem which has come down to us in the *Carmina Burana*, the poet writes that he has been caught by the hook of love:

> Ergo solus solam amo
> cuius captus sum ab hamo,
> nec vicem reciprocat . . .[70]

[10-12]

Therefore, I love one single girl, by whose hook I have been captured, but she gives no love in return.

By using the image of the hook (*hamus*), the poet has established his captive condition as a part of the very nature of things. The usage is more complex than simple poetic imagery. "*Amo*" (1st person, sing., indic.), the concept goes, "and *therefore* I am caught by the (*h*)*amo*" (ablative sing., with silent *h*). The poet could hardly have expressed his amorous captivity more essentially. This kind of meaning, derived from a supposed etymological connection between *amare* and *hamus*, goes back at least to Isidore of Seville. Although not making the link with *hamus* in his discussion of *amor*, as one might have expected, Isidore does do so under *amicus*:

amicus ab hamo, id est, a catena caritatis; unde et hami quod teneant.[71]

70. Whicher, p. 188.
71. *Etymologies*, X.5.

[47]

friend from *hook*; i.e., from the chains of divine love; and also because hooks hold.

The idea becomes a medieval commonplace, and echoes of Isidore are heard throughout the Middle Ages. Thus Andreas Capellanus makes use of it in the famous *De arte honesti amandi*:

> Dicitur autem amor ab amo verbo, quod significat capere vel capi. Nam qui amat, captus est cupidinis vinculis aliumque desiderat suo capere hamo. Sicut enim piscator astutus suis conatur cibiculis attrahere pisces et ipsos sui hami capere unco, ita vero captus amore suis nititur alium attrahere blandimentis totisque nisibus instat duo diversa quodam incorporali vinculo corda unire vel unita semper coniuncta servare.[72]

> Love is called *amor* by relation to the word *hook*, which means "to capture" or "to be captured." For whoever is in love is captured by the chains of desire, and himself wishes to capture someone else with his own hook. For just as a skilful fisherman tries to attract fish with his baits and capture them with his barbed hook, so does the captive of love strive to attract another with his flattery, and, putting forth all his efforts, seeks to unite two different hearts with an intangible chain or, if already united, to preserve them so forever.

Like the Latin lyric, John Peacham rhymes *amo* with *hamo*. Yet his is no mere *hamus amoris*, nor, with Andreas Capellanus, a *vinculum cupidinis*. Rather, by an audacious turn of the image, Peacham has made it into the *hamus caritatis* which Christ himself voluntarily swallowed in order to bring salvation to mankind:

> Ista signa recolens
> oci, oci clamo,
> Dulcis Iesu, querula,
> quod te minus amo,
> Stringi tamen cupio
> disciplinae chamo,
> Sicut pro me captus es
> caritatis hamo.

[St. 55]

72. *De Amore*, ed. E. Trojel (Munich: Wilhelm Fink, 1964), p. 9.

Bearing in mind these signs, plaintively I cry *oci, oci*. All too little I love you, sweet Jesus, and so I desire to be restrained by the rein of discipline, just as you were captured by the hook of divine love for me.

At the same time, however, this hook of divine love is also a *hamus mortis*, "hook of death," for what Caritas offers is the hook of the cross, covered with the *esca placita* ("pleasing bait," St. 56) of man's salvation. Yet, again unlike Andreas's comparison with the deceiving hooks of the fisherman, here Christ is quite aware of the hook which lies hidden in the bait; nevertheless, because of his *desiderium escae* ("desire for the bait," St. 57), that is, his own great charity toward mankind, he rushes upon the *hamum* and is captured for love.

To an even greater extent than the *hamus amoris*, the hook of the cross is, for the Middle Ages, a literary, iconographic, and theological commonplace; and what Peacham has managed in the *Philomena praevia* is a merging and an absolute fusion of the two conventions. Yet a result of that fusion, the necessary changes having been made, is that the old convention emerges renewed and transformed. In order to grasp the full extent of the change, however, it is necessary to understand the range of ideas which lie back of the hook of the cross; and perhaps the most readily accessible way into this realm is through the iconographic tradition. In the famous *Hortus deliciarum*, for example, there appears a miniature of Christ depicted on a hook-cross, which dangles before the head of the great Leviathan; the cross is attached to a line (the "line" of David), and the line is attached to a fishing pole held, apparently, by God the Father himself.[73] Here, clearly, Christ himself is the bait, and the great Leviathan, that is, Satan, is just on the point of being caught. This is the usual form that the image takes in the Middle Ages. "Canst thou draw out the leviathan with a hook," the Lord asks Job.[74] The Fathers of the Church very naturally understood this Leviathan as Satan; the one who was to capture him as Christ.

---

73. See *Hortus deliciarum*, ed. Joseph Walter (Strasbourg: Editeurs F-X Le Roux, 1952), plate XVIb.

74. Job XL.20. Douay-Rheims version.

Yet this still does not go very far, of course, toward explaining how Christ shows up in this miniature as the bait on the hook. The image, in fact, is grounded in an early theory of Redemption, which usually goes under the title of the Abuse of Powers theory. Briefly, the concept is as follows: as a result of original sin, Satan acquired certain legal rights over mankind, rights which could be abrogated only by Satan's overstepping his legal authority. Mankind had been made subject to death and hell through sin, but if a sinless man could be found over whom Satan would wrongfully assert his power of death, then the contract would be broken and mankind saved. Hence, Christ's entry into the world. Obviously, however, Satan must remain ignorant of Christ's identity, and thus is set in motion an elaborate scheme of holy deception: Christ is born of a virgin, to be sure, but a virgin deceptively betrothed to a man; Christ suffers hunger, thirst, heat, and cold like any ordinary man; the outcome of the Temptation of the Wilderness is left deliberately ambiguous so as to keep Satan in the dark, etc., etc. From this vantage point, it becomes a simple matter to interpret the *Hortus deliciarum* miniature. Christ's body is the tempting bait offered to an unsuspecting Satan. Hidden within that flesh, however, is the hook of divinity, and when the Leviathan swallows the bait, he strangles on the hook and vomits forth all of mankind. Another important element of the miniature is that the Christ depicted is a crowned, triumphant, conquering Saviour; there is no hint of suffering on his features. This is completely consonant, of course, with the Abuse of Powers theory, which presents the Redemption essentially as a contest of will and might between two great powers.

Under the influence, however, of the *Cur Deus Homo* of St. Anselm of Canterbury (d. 1109), the whole complex of ideas concerning the Redemption underwent a radical change. Since man had sinned infinitely in sinning against God, he was forever incapable of himself making adequate satisfaction for his sin and was forever unable to love God as a creature ought to love his Creator. Yet God still had love for His creature, and therefore sent His own Son as substitute sacrifice to make infinite satisfaction for man. The new emphasis was therefore on expiation, and thus on the sufferings that God as man bore for mankind.

It is for such reasons then that although the ancient image of the hook-cross has been retained in the *Philomena praevia*, it has been fused with the hook of love and completely transformed. And although the pleasing bait is still present, all traces of the old deception are not only absent but are specifically denied: Christ is fully aware of the hook that lies under the *placita esca*. Moreover, the image in its new form is superbly suited to the theme of the poem as a whole—the mystical love-death of the *devote âme*—for the hook which Christ rushes joyfully upon is the hook of death, as well as the hook of the cross and the hook of divine love. And so it is that the nightingale/soul cries out *oci* in pain at her too little love for God and wishes to be nailed to the cross with Him, for only by being crucified with the Christ can she achieve total union with Him. It is this consummation which is achieved in the mystical love/death at the end of the poem.

One further image requires discussion. At the end of Stanza 70, the poet writes that the soul is brought back to the right way by the attraction of the bloody body of Christ on the cross, just as the hawk is recalled by the red meat of the lure:

> Et sicut accipiter
> totus inescatur
> Super carnem rubeam,
> per quam revocatur.
>
> [St. 70]

Just as the hawk is completely filled and satisfied by the red meat which has lured him back.

The conception may seem a strange, strained image, but it is not an unusual one. It is worked out in great detail, for example, in a late Middle English poem, where everything is made rather crudely explicit:

> Also take hede to þis ensawmpyl here
> þat is lykend vn-to þe fawconnere:
> þe whilk, when hes hawke fro hym dos fle,

[51]

Schews to þe hawke rede flesche to see.
And when þe hawke lokis þer vn-to,
Fast to his mayster he hastes to go.
þus do on Criste, as 3e may see
Hynges bledyng opon a tre,
Hys body with blody woundes schewynge
For to reduce to hym mans saule & brynge:
þe whilk from hym by syn dos fle a-way,
And to hym will turne agayn with-outen delay.
þus he has his armes spred, man to hals & kysse,
þat to hym by luf wil turne, repentyng his mys.[75]

Moreover, a carved angel of the thirteenth century at Lincoln Cathedral seems also linked with the tradition. Appearing among a group of figures, all of which embody some particular meaning, the angel holds a hawk which is tearing at a large piece of meat, a scene which is apparently intended to symbolize the crucifixion.[76]

At all events, the image was quite well known to the French translator of the *Philomena praevia*, for he greatly expanded the brief, passing simile that Peacham had used, and devoted two full stanzas to it:

Peu pense pecheur de bien faire retrait,
Pour quoy dius nous monstra son coeur par doulz attrait
Sur l'esle de la croix; ne ne pense le trait,
Car c'est le reclain qui le faucon attrait.

Quanteffoiz que cest leurre est par désir veus
Tant de foiz coeur piteux est de menger meus,
Et ainsi com l'oisel est par la char reus
Est le coeur se du sang Jhésus est repeus.

[St. 69-70]

75. See Thomas W. Ross, "Five Fifteenth-Century 'Emblem' Verses from Brit. Mus. Addit. MS. 37049," *Speculum*, 32 (1957), 278-79. For a wide-ranging and detailed discussion of the hawk-lure complex as an image of sexual love, as well as love of the soul for the crucified Christ, see J. L. Baird and Garrett McCutchan, "Love, Lures, Hawks, and the Gentle Art of Translation," *Italica*, 53 (1976), 236-47.

76. See M. D. Anderson, *Drama and Imagery in English Medieval Churches* (Cambridge: Cambridge University Press, 1963), pp. 1-2.

In Stanza 69 Peacham had used the image of the bed of his heart which Christ offers from the cross to sinful mankind. For whatever reason—perhaps Peacham's *reclinatorium* "bed" reminded him of his own *reclain* "lure"[77]—the French poet has changed all this, and his version is a great improvement upon the Latin. In contrast to Peacham's rather esoteric and ethereal imagery of the bed of Christ's heart, an idea which, in any case, tails off rather aimlessly into the hawk image, the French poet has centered all the material in the stark hawk-lure metaphor and has made it work poetically.

JLB

77. The French translator was not, in any case, the only one who felt the need for beginning the hawk image earlier. Five of the twelve Latin MSS. collated by Dreves give a reading of *reclamatorium* "lure," "a re-calling"? in both instances where *reclinatorium* occurs in Stanza 70 of the edited text. The translator may, of course, have had a MS. which gave the reading *reclamatorium*; if so, the *reclinatorium* of Stanza 69 was also probably affected (as in his translation), which is not true, however, of any of the collated MSS.

Appendix

John Peacham

John Peacham (Peckam, Pecham) was quite a notable man of his time, the second half of the thirteenth century. He once served as regent master of theology at the University of Paris, during the second regency of Thomas Aquinas; he participated in the defense of the mendicant orders against the famous antifraternal attack spearheaded by William of St. Amour; he served as master of the Franciscans at Oxford; he became archbishop of Canterbury in 1279. Peacham was an Englishman and, in fact, takes his name from the village of Patcham in Sussex. He was educated at Oxford and Paris, and at one point sat under the great Bonaventure, interestingly in light of the fact that his *Philomena praevia* was long attributed to the seraphic doctor. Peacham joined the Franciscan Order about 1250. He taught at both Oxford and the University of Paris, and he died on December 8, 1292.[78]

The Manuscript

The *Rossignol* has come down to us in a single MS. of the fifteenth century, now housed in the British Library as MS. Egerton 2834. The MS. is of paper and is quite small, containing only thirty-eight folios, measuring 11-1/4 in. x 8 in. In the sixteenth century the MS. belonged to Jean le Feron of Charleville, priest at Compiègne. Thus folio 32 contains the words, "Ex libris Jo. Feronei Carolopolitani sac. Compendiensis," and folio 38b, "Pour M. Jehan de Feron." The only item in the MS., other than the *Rossignol*, is the *Testament* of Jean de Meun, with which the MS. opens. The *Rossignol* begins on folio 34 with the heading "Ensieut le traictiet du roussignol oyselet amoureux."

The language of the MS. is fairly standard northern French, with a few surprisingly early forms preserved and with some

---

78. See J. C. Russell, *Dictionary of Writers of Thirteenth Century England* (1936; New York: Burt Franklin, 1971).

[55]

admixture of forms which may be owing to the influence of the Picard dialect. There is little consistency, however, so that the palatalization of Latin *k* to *ch* before *e* (as in Picard) also shows up in the regular form with the sibilant *c*: *doucher*, St. 23, l. 1, but *doulceur*, St. 29, l. 1; *chest*, St. 53, l. 2, but *cest*, St. 32, l. 1 and St. 70, l. 1; and *tierche*, St. 8, l. 1, but *tierce*, St. 35, l. 2. The palatalization does not, however, occur before *i*, as one might expect; thus *cilz*, *cy*, but never *chilz*, etc. In any case, the palatal *ch* was apparently not pronounced as such, since Stanza 30 contains rhymes in *-ice*, with *nourice*, *vice*, and *office*, all rhyming with *niche*. A very striking petrified form is *enfes*, which preserves the early declensional forms quite regularly: thus *enfes* (vocative sing.), St. 29, l. 1 and (nom. sing.), St. 31, l. 1, but *enfant* (acc. sing.), St. 30, l. 2. Similarly, the MS. preserves *chans* (nom. sing.), St. 11, l. 3, but *chant* (acc. sing.), St. 12, l. 4; St. 7, l. 3; St. 9, l. 2. Other early forms are *il ont* (for *ils ont*), St. 44, l. 2; and *mi frere* (for *mon frere*), St. 87, l. 1.

The poem is written in quatrains, rhyming a a a a, with stanza groupings being consistently maintained throughout. Each line begins with a capital, with larger, more prominent capitals being used to introduce new quatrains. Aside from such clearly marked verse-grouping—and each quatrain is a self-contained unit of meaning—the scribe has made no attempt at punctuation. All marks of punctuation have been supplied by the editors, including the apostrophe in such a grouping, for example, as *c'est*. The scribe has made use throughout of numerous, though quite standard forms of abbreviation, and these have been silently expanded by the editors. The most commonly abbreviated words in the MS. are the following: *et*, *que*, *qui*, *jour* (=*ur* abbreviation, which occurs with a number of words of this type, including *amour*), *Jhesus*, *propre*, *proprement*. Words marked for nasalization have also been silently expanded. As usual, the most difficult problem in reading the MS. is caused by the *i* plus nasal combinations. The scribe has frequently, though not consistently, been of assistance here by his use of a thin diagonal line over the *i*. Accent marks have also been supplied by the editors.

[56]

Ossignol messager damoureuse nouuelle
Qui congnois la saison du temps quand renouuelle
Qui le cueur estoye par tarhanson tad belle
Je te pry humblement vien a moy qui tappelle
Vien vien se ten vas ou je aler ne puys
Mon amy salueras par tes chans pl[...]
Et son cueur ostrae les doleurs ...
Trop me desplaut helas sy pres de luy me ...
A tes auguement doulz oyse je te prie
Salue mon amy a qui je suy amie
Et luy dis que ma joye mon soulas z ma vye
Et quant a luy serons mon cueur si sestendre
Et sauons demandoyent pour quoy je ten ...
Dis luy sauve mon messange sachent que jay len
De toy propprietes rien escript dea
Va dieu soit aggreable z je say bien san
Et dont ame dnote mit en ton entente
Car se tu veulz garder de cest oysel la sente
Tu porras desseruir en la vie presente
Pur le chant du ciel sauon come on lasente
Ce ad lamoureux oysel veult en chant faisonner
Sus monte il sur laubre s porro mieuz entoner
Tent le bec au ceur pour ylorre adieu donner
Si quil fait par son chant tout le bois resonner
Son chant doulz replaisant laube du jour saline
Mais quant plus vient auant que prime est venne

The MS. is written in a bold, clearly legible hand by a careful scribe, and poses few problems for the editor. Only two minor emendations of the text were required: in Stanza 35, line 4, the *donne* of the MS. has been expanded by the editors to *donner*, with the final *r* being placed in brackets; the *char* of Stanza 78, line 4 represents an emended form of MS. *chart*. These emendations receive notice in the Notes to the edition.

The Nightingale

Rossignol

Rossignol, messager d'amoureuse nouvelle,   *1*
Qui cognois la saison du temps quant renouvelle,
Qui le coeur esioys par ta chanson tant belle,
Je te pry humblement, vien à moy qui t'appele.

Vien, vien, si t'en iras ou je aler ne puys;   *2*
Mon amy salueras par tes chans et déduys,
De son coeur ostras les doleurs et ennuys,
Trop me desplait, hélas, que pres de luy ne suys.

Va tos légierement, doulz oysel, je te prie,   *3*
Salue moy celuy à qui je suy amie,
Et ly dis que ma joye, mon soulas, et ma vye
Est quant à luy servir mon coeur si s'estudye.

Et s'aucuns demandoyent pour quoy je t'ay esleu   *4*
Pour faire mon messaige, sachent que j'ay leu
De toy propriétez et en escript veu
Qu'à dieu sont aggréables et je l'ay bien sceu.

Or donc, ame dévote, met cy ton entente,   *5*
Car se tu veulz garder de cest oysel la sente,
Tu porras desservir en la vie présente,
Oyr le chant du chiel, savoir comme on l'ascente.

Quant l'amoureux oysel veult en chant foisonner,   *6*
Adonc monte il sur l'arbre, et pour mieux entonner
Il tent le bec au vent pour gloire à dieu donner,
Si qu'il fait par son chant tout le bois résonner.

The Nightingale

O nightingale, bearer of love's news,   *1*
O harbinger of the spring season,
You who gladden hearts with your sweet song,
Come, I beg of you, come to me, I pray.

Come, that I may send you where I cannot go,   *2*
To greet my beloved with your delightful songs,
And lift from his heart his suffering and pain;
Alas, how sad I am to be so far from him.

Go blithely, sweet bird, I pray,   *3*
Take him greetings from me, his lady love,
And tell him that my joy, my happiness and my life
All consist in my desire to serve him with all my heart.

And if anyone should ask why I have chosen you   *4*
To take my message, let him know that I have read
Of your qualities and have learned to my satisfaction
That they are pleasing to God.

Now, devout soul, seek to understand,   *5*
For if you are willing to follow this bird's path,
You will be able to free yourself from this earthly life,
Hear the music of heaven, and learn how to ascend there.

For when the bird of love wishes to pour forth its song,   *6*
It flies to a tree-top and stretches its beak
To the wind to sing more loudly to the glory of God;
Thus does the wood resound with its song.

D'un chant doulz et plaisant l'aube du jour salue,   7
Mais quant plus vient avant que prime est venue,
Adonc mue il son chant en musique menue,
Ne ne repose nient ains tousiours continue.

Envers l'eure de tierche à maniere oublyee,   8
Car la chaleur du jour a sa joye doublee
La gorge à peu li ront tant est la voix montee,
Et com plus chante fort tant plus en est tempïee.

A l'eure de miedy que le solail se hauche,   9
Les vaines li derompent tant forment son chant hauche;
"Ocy, ocy," escrie à vive voix non fausse,
Dont il pert tout son chant et son plaisant chant fausse.

Quant elle a tant chanté que sa voix en est mue,   10
Elle remuet le bec, tout le corps ly tressue,
Quant vient l'eure de nonne de mort elle est vainque;
Elle n'a vaine ou corps qui ne luy soit rompue.

Or donc, ame dévote, tu as oy briefment   11
Le fait de cest oysel et son dégoisement,
Mais j'ay dit pardevant que cilz chans proprement
Si poeut estre appliquié à nostre sauvement.

Saches de cest oysel tient la similitude   12
L'ame qui en dieu aimer met toute son estude,
Qui quant de lasus pense la grant béatitude,
Elle compose un chant de musique non rude.

Pour accroistre de l'âme la foy et l'espérance,   13
Luy est monstré un jour et en segnefiance,
Que les heures du jour font à nous congnoissance
Des biens que recepvons de dieu en habondance.

[64]

It greets the dawn with a sweet and pleasing song,   7
But as time passes and Prime arrives,
It changes its song into a minor key
And never ceases for the whole of the day.

Then near the hour of Tierce it sings a long-lost tune,   8
For the heat of the day so increases its joy
That its throat almost bursts with its wild notes,
And the more it sings the more strenuous its efforts become.

At Midday when the sun is at its height,   9
It lifts its note so high that all its veins burst,
As it cries "Oci, oci," in its true and vibrant voice;
Thus its song fades and loses its pleasant tone.

And when it has sung so vigorously that it can sing no
    more,   10
It shakes its beak, all its body drenched with sweat,
And as the hour of Nones arrives, it is finally conquered by
    death,
With every vein in its body burst asunder.

Now, devout soul, you have briefly heard   11
The properties of this bird and its song.
But, as I said before, this song
Can fittingly be applied to our salvation.

You should know that this bird is the figure   12
Of the soul who puts all its effort into loving God.
And from its great height, remembering its blessings,
Composes a most harmonious hymn.

For the significance and the meaning of one day   13
Are revealed to the soul to increase its faith and hope,
Because the Hours make us aware of the great good
Which we receive abundantly from God.

[65]

Nostre commencement est dit l'aube journee,   14
Quant adam fust crées et eve fust formee;
Prime quant fut marie de l'angle saluee;
Et tierche fust l'aage de Jésus trespassee.

Midi quant des felons se vault lessier lyer,   15
Batre et vilener, tourmenter, decracher,
Et des juifs pervers tant durement traictier,
Pendre honteusement et le coste percher.

Nonne quant Jhésus Christ a l'esperit hors mis,   16
Quant il eust fait le cours qui luy estoit commis,
Et il eust l'ennemi combatu et sousmis;
Vespre quant il fust de la croix jus demis.

Adès l'ame dévote qui a oy l'istoyre   17
Ne met rien en oubly; ains pour avoir mémoire,
Elle monte sur l'arbre ou Jhésus ot victoire
De nostre adversaire pour nous donner sa gloire.

Tantos la voix du coeur dévotement eslieve   18
En commenchant son chant quant l'aube du jour crieve,
Glorefie et loe dieu par sa chanson non brieve,
Et pour luy gracier de hault chanter s'engrieve.

°   "Créateur véritable, quant fus de toy cree,   19
Ta pitié souveraine donc fust démonstree,
Que l'ame de ta gloire sera en fin doee,
Qui à toy se conjoint et de toy est amee.

17.3 Jhésus. *Leo fortis* in the Latin. If the translator has lost something by
substituting the name for the image, he has in the next line at least
improved upon the inharmonious staccato effect of the Latin *fractis
mortis portis.*

Matins signifies our beginning,   14
When Adam was created and Eve was formed;
Prime signifies the Annunciation;
And Tierce signifies the manhood of Jesus.

Midday is the time when Christ permitted his enemies   15
To bind, beat, flog, torment, and spit upon him,
And allowed the perverse Jews to handle him roughly,
To hang him shamefully and to pierce his side.

Nones signifies the time when Jesus Christ gave up the
    ghost,   16
Once he had completed the task entrusted to him
And utterly defeated the enemy.
Vespers, when he was taken down from the cross.

The devout soul who has heard the story   17
Forgets nothing: rather, to preserve the moment,
She promptly mounts the tree on which Jesus
Triumphed over our adversary to give us his glory.

At once she devoutly raises the voice of her heart,   18
As she begins her song at Matins;
Glorifying and praising God in her extended song
And straining to lift up her voice in thanks to God.

"O true Creator, your supreme mercy was displayed   19
When you created me; for the soul which joins itself
To you and is loved by you,
Will finally be endowed with your glory.

Quant honneur me donnas et à tout mon lignage—   20
La saincte trinité qu'en moy mist son ymaige—
Assez fusse plus noble se n'eusses eu coeur volaige,
Quant trespassay la loy de dieu par mon oultrage.

Car tu, vraye charité, avoec toy allyer   21
Me voloyes du tout et moy acompaigner,
Et en ton doulz hostel doulcement herbergier,
Et moy sicom ta fille nourrir et ensegner.

Dès adonc pensas tu que conioincte seroye   22
A cheulx qu'en toy loer prennent parfaicte joye;
Tout est tien: je n'ay rien quy soit mien que je voye
Que te puisse donner se m'amour ne t'otroye.

Doucher et charité, de tous biens souffissance,   23
Des vrais coeurs amoureux singlier alliance,
Tout quanques j'ay vaillant en mondaine sustance,
Et mon corps et mon âme, met en ton ordonnance."

"Ocy," chante tel coeur qui s'esioyt en paine,   24
Et dist que cest bien droit que créature humaine
Aime de coeur l'ouvrier et de pensee saine,
Qui ainsi le vault créer et d'ignoscence plaine.

Ainsi l'aube du jour passe l'ame dévote;   25
A prime est transportee en enforchant sa notte,
Et pense à cest doulz tamps et bien en son coeur notte
Quant dieux vint pour vestir d'umain corps l'umble coste.

20.3 **coeur volaige.** "Flighty heart" seems nicely suited to the nightin-
gale/soul. Cf. the Latin, which employs no image at all: *Nisi iussum
Domini fuissem transgressa.*

[68]

When you bestowed honor on me and on my lineage   20
—the Holy Trinity placed its image upon me—
I would have been noble indeed had I not,
Through my flighty heart, transgressed Divine Law by my
    iniquities.

For, O true Charity, you wished to bind me to you utterly, 21
To be with me always, to lodge me
In your sweet mansion
And to nourish and teach me as your daughter.

Then you intended me to be joined with those   22
Who find perfect joy in praising you;
And since all things are yours, I have nothing
Of my own to give you, save my love.

Sweetness and Charity, Abundance of all goodness,   23
Unique Bond of true loving hearts,
All that I have in worldly goods, both my body
And my soul, I place in your governance."

Rejoicing in its pain, such a heart sings, "Oci,"   24
And says that it is truly fitting for a human creature
To love with mind and spirit the Maker who
Chose to create her full of innocence.

The devout soul passes the hour of Matins in this way.   25
At Prime she is in ecstasy as she raises her song,
While contemplating that sweet time when God
Came to dress himself in the humble cloak of human flesh.

L'ame ainsi se remue par vraye charité   26
Et tramble quant voit dieu en tel nécessité,
Plourer comme un enfant selon humanité,
Pour hoster son sergant de son adversité.

En plourant li demande, "Dieu, de pitié fontaine,   27
Qui t'a vestu ma robe tant povre et tant vileine?
Qui te donna conseil de faire à nous estraine
De ton corps fors amour et charité soueraine?

Par droit est telle amour forte et ardant nommee,   28
Par qui déité prise fust et emprisonnee,
Et en ses fors lyens lyee et enfermee,
Et des draps d'un enfant povre envelopee.

Enfes qui es sans per, O de doulceur vivier,   29
Eureux fust qui adonc accoler et baisier
Te peust pies et mains et en toy soulacier,
Adonc estre avoec toy me fust tresgrant loyer.

Las moy, que ne fus je eslite pour nourrice   30
De ce petit enfant, filz de vierge sans vice;
Bien l'eusse nourry, jasoye je bien niche;
Touiours fusse à son bers sans faire autre office.

Je croy que li doulx enfes n'eust ja mot sonné   31
Se un povre l'eust couchiet pris et arraisonné;
Ains eust sicom l'enfant un doulcet ris donné
Et à tous repentans de leger pardonné.

31.4 repentans. A mistranslation? The Latin has at this point: *Et petenti veniam facile faveret*, "And would easily grant the favor to the one who sought it."

The soul is excited by true charity   26
And trembles at seeing God in such a parlous state,
Weeping like a child in his humanity
In order to liberate his servant from his misfortune.

And weeping, she asks him: "O God, Fountain of mercy,   27
Who dressed you in my poor and lowly robe?
Who advised you to make us the gift of your body?
Who, if not love and supreme charity?

Rightly such a love is called powerful and burning   28
By which even God himself was taken and imprisoned,
Bound and held captive in its strong bonds,
And wrapped in the swaddling clothes of a poor child.

O peerless child, O fountain of sweetness!   29
He who could embrace you, kiss your hands and feet,
And take comfort in you would be fortunate indeed.
And for me to be with you would be a splendid reward.

Alas, why was I not chosen as nurse of this little child,   30
The Son of the spotless Virgin!
I would have nursed him well, ignorant though I am;
I would have been constantly by his cradle, scorning all
    other tasks.

I think that the sweet child would not have complained   31
If some poor soul had picked him up as he lay and had
    spoken to him,
But rather, like a little child, would have given a sweet smile
And readily forgiven all those who repent.

Eureux fust qui à cest temps peust à sa mere embastre   32
Si dévote priere que, par sa coulpe battre,
Elle eust conget donné d'une foiz ou de quatre
Baisier son chier enfant et avoec luy esbatre.

O com de coeur entier un baing li attrempasse!   33
Com volentiers l'yaue à mon col portasse!
Et a sa doulce mere de coeur administrasse
Et du petit enfant les drappelles lavasse!"

Si désire povre estre l'ame de pechiet monde,   34
Vilté et abstinence en son hostel habonde;
Tout labour luy est mue en joye tresparfonde,
Ne ne tient qu'à vilté tout l'onneur de cest monde.

Et quant de Jhesus Christ a l'enfance chanté,   35
Prime a fait son cours; tierce vient à plenté,
Si chante la chanson ou a son coeur planté
Des paines qu'il souffri pour nous donne[r] sancté.

Si recorde en son coeur la paine qu'a soufferte,   36
Sueur, froideur, chaleur, fam, soif, sans sa desserte,
Pour humaine nature qui tant estoit déserte,
Affin que d'obéir à dieu fust plus apperte.

Si art, cuyt, et enflambe, tant en est dolereuse,   37
"Ocy, ocy," escrie telle ame glorieuse;
Morir o monde quiert pour estre à dieu espeuse;
Tout bien mondain refuse tant est délicieuse.

35.4 donne[r]. MS. *donne.*

[72]

Fortunate would he be who could address to the child's
    mother   32
An urgent prayer, a prayer so devout that, hearing his "Mea
    Culpa,"
She would grant him permission
To kiss and play time and again with her dear child.

O how cheerfully I would have prepared his bath for him, 33
How gladly I would have carried the water on my back,
And how happily I would have ministered to his sweet
    mother,
And even have washed the child's tiny clothes."

Thus does the sinless soul desire to be humble;   34
Lowliness and abstemiousness govern his household;
Thus every menial task is transformed into deepest joy,
And, for her, every worldly honor is vile.

By the time she has fully recounted the infancy of Christ
    in song,   35
The hour of Prime has passed and Tierce has arrived;
Then, with a full heart, she sings
Of the sufferings he bore for our salvation.

The sweat, the cold, the heat, the hunger, and the thirst, 36
All these she remembers in her heart, the sufferings
That he bore blamelessly for a hapless and lost humanity,
That man might learn again to obey God.

Thus does it burn, blaze, and seethe in its great anguish, 37
Such a glorious soul, crying, "Oci, oci,"
Seeking to die to this world, to be espoused to God,
Spurning all worldly things in her rapture.

Si parle à son seigneur, "O amoureux espoux,   38
Des esgarez refuge, des povres herbergourx,
Qui es des pénitens singuliers confortourx,
Aprez toy doibt courir et justes et pécheourx.

Aux justes, quel merveille rigle est a ta doctrine!   39
Des pécheurs, es miroir de vie discipline;
Aux traveilles, repos qui tout labeur affine;
Aux povres langoureux, souveraine médecine.

Tu fus le premier qui vault amor preescher   40
Et dis que on doit ta gloire seulement avoir chier;
Tu seus de cest monde la molle descharger
Pour plus pres de l'estoile perdue approcher.

Et les juifs pervers, qui touiours sont despis,   41
S'en moquoyent et disoyent qu'en toy n'est nulz respis,
Mais tu, vraye bonté, ne rendis pas au pis;
Ains de coeur pardonnoyes pour mettre main au pis.

C'est bien drois, car ton nom est de compassion,   42
Qui désire estre amé sans domination,
Qui sans nul menacher preeschoyes dilection,
Qui fins révérence et preis abjection.

38.2, 3, 4 herbergourx, confortourx, pecheourx. The X's here are indeed
in the MS., employed apparently to preserve sight-rhyme.

40.4 l'estoile perdue approcher. At this point the Latin reads *rehabere
stolam*. It seems inescapable that the translator had a corrupt text
before him, in which *stolam* "robe" had been replaced by *stellam* "star."
The *Analecta Hymnica* edition does not, however, note this form in any
of the collated MSS.

41.4 pour. Read *par*.

[74]

Then she addresses her Lord in these words: "O loving
   husband,   38
Refuge for those gone astray, almoner for the poor,
O unique comforter for the penitent,
The just and the sinful alike should hasten to seek you.

For the just, what a wonderful rule of life your doctrine
   is!   39
For sinners, you are the mirror in which they may see the
   virtuous life,
For laborers, you are the rest which brings all work to an end,
For those who languish in poverty, the sovereign remedy.

You were the first who chose to preach of love,   40
And who insisted that man should cherish only your glory,
Through you, man was enabled to disburden himself
From the mill-stone of this world and approach again the
   lost star.

And the perverse Jews who are always despised   41
Mocked your words, saying there is no forgiveness in you,
But you, True Goodness, did not render evil for evil;
Rather you pardoned fully by taking evil upon yourself.

Such is entirely fitting, for your very name stands for
   compassion,   42
You who desire to be loved with a free and unforced love,
You who without constraint taught love,
And who valued humility and proper reverence.

[75]

De la femme forfante grant probation as   43
Que ta pitié est grande quant l'arraisonnas,
La magdalene aussi à cuy tu pardonnas
Les vii pechies mortelz, et grace luy donnas.

Et que puys-je plus dire? Tous cheulx qui l'ont ensuyt   44
Et sa fourme de vivre il ont péchiet destruyt
Et sont en bonnes moeurs et nourry et aduyt,
De l'ennemi seurs et en gloire conduyt.

Bien eures est cilz le quel sa vie toute   45
Use dessoubz tel maistre, et qui ensuit sa route,
Et sucche de sa bouche le miel qui en degouste,
Devant qui grant doulcheur est amer qui en gouste."

Et com l'ame dévote fait telle mélodie,   46
De rendre grace à dieu est toute apparellye,
En loant son seigneur est toudis enforchie,
Ainsi est la chansson de tierche défaillye.

"Ocy, ocy," escrie l'ame et derechief   47
Pleure et se complaint et est à grant meschief,
En plourant loe dieu qu'est de tout bien le chief,
Qui tant souffry pour nous et pour nostre meschief.

A chelle heure l'ame samble toute enyvree,   48
Mais quant la grant chaleur de miedi est montee,
Adonc de la sayecte d'amours est si navree
Que la mort de Jhésus met toute en sa pensee.

43.1 femme forfante. "Sinful woman." The Latin more precisely indicates that this is the Woman taken in Adultery: *adulterio . . . deprehensa.*

47.4 meschief. Crossed through and replaced, apparently by the same hand, with the word *pechiet*, thereby sacrificing the rhyme *-ief*.

You gave proof how great your mercy is   43
When you brought the woman caught in adultery back to
    the right way,
Just as you forgave the Magdalene for the seven deadly sins,
And gave your grace to her.

What more can I say? All those who have followed him   44
And his governance have conquered sin,
And have been sustained in the good life,
Safe from the enemy, and have been led into glory.

Happy is he who spends all his life   45
Under such a master, following his path,
And is able to suck the honey that drips from his lips,
Compared with which all earthly sweetness tastes bitter."

As the devout soul sings such a melody   46
With her whole heart sending forth thanks to God,
She is ever more strengthened in praising her Lord:
Thus does the song of Tierce come to an end.

"Oci, oci!" the soul cries,   47
Weeping and lamenting in great distress
And, in weeping, praises her God who is the fountain of all
    good,
Who suffered so greatly for our misfortune.

At this hour the soul seems intoxicated in its ecstasy,   48
But as the great heat of Midday arrives,
She is then so wounded by the arrow of love
That she turns her whole thought to the death of Jesus.

En plourant voit l'aignel pour nostre achoisonné,   49
L'aignel voit sans malice d'espines couronné,
De cheux agus perchiet, playet, emprisonné,
Et tout le corps de luy de sang environné.

"Ocy," adonc escrie mil foiz par grant ardure,   50
"Ocy, ocy, las, moy! Il n'est voix qui luy dure
Quant voit de son amy la face tant obscure
Pour nous languir en croix et souffrir mort si dure.

Comment convenoit il que l'aignel tant bénigne   51
Fust mis à tel meschief et à mort tant indigne,
Bien croy que tout fust fait pour vaincre le maligne,
Et pour nous démonstre d'amour un certain signe.

Ce fut d'amour le signe qui les derrains attaindre   52
Fist les premiers de vray, et le hault au bas joindre,
Et clerement monstra qu'il nous amoit sans faindre,
Quant lessa en son corps tant de playes empraindre.

'Tu es amy nouvel, tu es tresdelitable,'   53
Le sage ainsi t'appelle chest chos raisonnable;
'Tu degoustes tousdis et rent goust aggreable,
La char est le tonnel comme vaissel notable.'

50.2 **Ocy, ocy.** For the first time we translate the cry *oci* as the impera-
tive singular of the verb "to kill." The Latin is completely unambigu-
ous with its *Oci, oci miseram*, "Kill, kill wretched me." The French ver-
sion is less clear. The *moy* here could, of course, be simply a part of
the exclamation *las moy*, to be rendered simply "alas." But since the
French poet stays generally quite close to his Latin text and since the
context of the stanza seems to demand it, we feel it necessary to
take *moy* as the object of *oci*.

[78]

She weeps as she sees the lamb—   49
The guileless lamb, crowned with thorns,
Pierced by nails, wounded and bound captive,
His whole body covered with blood—all for our guilt.

Then she cries "Oci" a thousand times in her burning
    ardor: 50
"Alas, kill, kill me! What voice would hold up
Under the strain of seeing one's beloved languishing
For us on the cross, with a livid face, suffering so harsh a
    death!

How could it be that such a gentle lamb   51
Should be subjected to such a misfortune and such an
    unworthy death?
All this was done, I know, in order to conquer the Evil One,
And to give us a clear token of his great love.

This was the sign of love which truly made the last first,   52
And brought down the mighty;
Clearly did he show how fully he loved us
When he allowed his body to be so cruelly wounded.

'You are a new lover, you are delectable,'   53
The wise man describes you thus and rightly so.
'Your flesh is like a wine-cask, a noble vessel,
Which drips wine always pleasing to the taste.'

Par telz signes veus doit l'ame pénitente   54
Croire comme de coeur à nous dieux se présente;
Si m'en recordray que Sathan ne me tempte,
C'est ce qui de pechie plus empesche l'entente.

Quant m'en souvient, je crye 'Ocy, ocy,' ad plain,   55
Et de ce que peu t'aime, doulx Jhésus, me complain;
Si désir que m'estraingnes de discipline le frain,
Si comme amour pour moy te ravist a son hain.

Tresbien te sceust un aim charité envoyer,   56
Quant te vault pour un homme à morir conseiller,
Mais l'aim soubz la viande plaisant sot bien mucher,
Quant te monstra que par ce debvoyes ames gaigner.

Mais toutes foiz de l'aim broyes tu bien la poincte,   57
La quelle ne te fist onques ne paour ne craincte;
Ains d'aler contre luy fust ta volenté saincte,
La quelle par désir fus de menger contraincte.

Donques pour moy meschant que tu as tant amee,   58
Mordis en l'aguillon ou tu as mort trouvee,
Quant de toy à ton pere feis offrande sacree,
Et moy tresvile et orde fus en ton sang lavee.

Se je pour toy souspire, hélas, qui s'en merveille,   59
Qui suy conioincte à toy d'une amour non pareille;
Ta maniere m'attrait et mon désir esveille,
Quant pour moy souffris mort c'est à oyr merveilles.

56.2 un homme. One would expect the more generalized *l'homme*. The Latin reads *pro homine*.

By seeing such tokens any penitent soul   54
Will have to believe how generously God offers himself
    to us;
I shall bear such tokens in mind so that Satan may not tempt
    me,
For such memories are the best barrier against sin.

And when I remember these things, I cry aloud 'Oci, oci!'   55
Thus lamenting that I love you all too little, sweet Jesus,
And yearn to be restrained with the bridle of your discipline,
Just as Love captured you with her hook, for my sake.

Love knew very well how to cast a hook to you,   56
When she wished to talk you into dying for mankind,
But she also knew how to hide the hook under pleasing bait,
When she demonstrated to you that in this way you could win
    souls.

And so you bit freely upon the pointed hook,   57
Which you did not fear at all,
But rather you chose full willingly to rush upon it,
For, through your great desire, you were impelled to swallow
    the hook.

It was because you loved me so much, wicked as I was,   58
That you bit on this hook wherein you found death:
In this way you offered yourself as a holy sacrifice to your
    father,
And washed away my vileness and my filth in your blood.

Who would marvel if I, alas, sigh for you,   59
For I am joined to you by a peerless love;
Your courtesy attracts me and awakens my desire;
Your suffering death for me, that is a marvellous fact.

[81]

Vrayement je ne dois pas seulement souspirer,   60
Ains dois toute ma char avoec Job deschirer,
En la playe du coste bien mon nit atirer,
Et la mon esperit en doleur expirer.

Jhésus, s'en toy ne muyr point, ne reposeray;   61
'Ocy, ocy,' criant jamais ne chesseray;
Tousiours en ce propos fu et suy et seray,
Pour la honte du monde ja ne m'en ostray."

Or dit à l'oiseleur qu'il la prengne en ses las: 62
"Attache moy en croix lès mon amy, hélas!
De plus vivre n'ay cure, morir est mon soulas,
Fors que accoler te puisse sicomme m'accolas.

Autrement appaisie ja ne sera ma rage,   63
Par quoy mon coeur languist tousiours et est en rage,
Se toy qui es le puys de doulcheur et rivaige
Ne mes sur ma langueur chose qui l'assouage.

Car tu es le vray mire qui gairis sans pointure,   64
Qui sces oster du coeur doulcement toute ordure,
Car cheulx que tu veulx prendre en t'amour et en cure
Veulz oindre de tes mains et donner nourreture.

Las, com le monde tent à son grant dampnement,   65
Qui de ses ennemis tourmentes durement
Ne fait force du mire qui pour son sauvement
Fist fendre son coste tant amoureusement.

Indeed, I must not only sigh,   60
But like Job must mortify my flesh,
Build my nest in the wound of your side,
And there breathe forth my soul in sorrow.

Jesus, unless I die in you, I will never find rest: 61
I will cry out forever, 'Oci, oci,'
For this was, is, and always will be my intent,
And, because of the shamefulness of this world, I will never
    change it."

Then she tells the bird-catcher to capture her with his
    nets: 62
"Affix me, alas, to the cross beside my beloved,
For I wish to live no longer; dying is my only solace,
Save being able to embrace my beloved as he embraces
    me.

Otherwise my frenzy, which causes my heart always to
    suffer   63
And languish will never be stilled,
Unless you, the fountain and well of sweetness, apply
A soothing ointment to my languor.

For you are the true doctor who cures without the lancet,   64
And, gently, can purify the heart of all its filth,
And those whom you choose to take in your loving care
You sustain and anoint with your own hands.

Alas! how the world seeks its own undoing,   65
For, in the cruel grip of its enemy,
It fails to call upon the doctor
Who lovingly let his side be pierced for its salvation.

[83]

'Homme, qui n'as memoire de si grant bénefice   66
Que Jhésus Christ te fist quant morut pour ton vice;
Par sa mort fust rompu le las de grant malice;
Par sa mort te donna Jhésus toute délice.

Il de son propre corps te vault rassasier,   67
Et en son propre sang et laver et baingnier;
Son doulz corps vault à toy descouvrir despouiller
Pour demonstrer comment et combien t'avoit chier.'

O com, vees cy, doulz baing! O com souef viande!   68
Tu es la clef du chiel à coeur qui te demande;
A cheulx qui te rechoipvent n'est nulle paine grande,
Se n'est aux pescheux qu'oiseusette truande.

Peu pense pecheur de bien faire retrait,   69
Pour quoy dius nous monstra son coeur par doulz attrait
Sur l'esle de la croix; ne ne pense le trait,
Car c'est le reclain qui le faucon attrait.

Quanteffoiz que cest leurre est par désir veus   70
Tant de foiz coeur piteux est de menger meus,
Et ainsi com l'oisel est par la char reus
Est le coeur se du sang Jhésus est repeus."

Adonc brait et crie l'ame comme desvee,   71
"O leurre, O doulce char par tout ensanglantee,
Par tant de lieux batue, tresperchie, et navree,
Que ne suy avoec toy en croix à mort livree!

69.1-4 See Introduction, p. 53.

'O man, you forget the great boon   66
Which Jesus Christ bestowed on you when he died for
    your sins;
By his death, Jesus broke the bonds of wickedness;
By his death, he gave you every delight.

He desired to satisfy your hunger with his own body,   67
And to wash and bathe you with his own blood;
He was willing to lay his sweet body bare,
In order to demonstrate how fully and completely he loved
    you.'

O look, what a sweet bath! O what a delightful banquet!   68
You are the key of Heaven for the heart who seeks you,
For those who receive you there is no more suffering,
Though for sinners there is only miserable emptiness.

The sinner thinks all too little of the safe refuge   69
Which God tendered by showing us his heart as a sweet
    attraction
On the wing of the cross; nor does he heed the bait,
For this is the lure which attracts the falcon.

As often as this lure is seen with desire   70
So often is the pious heart moved to eat of it,
And just as the bird is recalled by the lure of the meat
So is the heart fully nourished by Christ's blood."

Then the soul shrieks and cries like one beside herself,   71
"O lure, O sweet flesh, covered with blood,
Beaten, pierced, and wounded all over your body,
Why was I not put on the cross to die with you!

[85]

Or ne poeut estre ainsi, si convient que je eslise 72
Nouvel crucefiement qu'à mon amy souffise:
Plourer veul et jémir quant de mon mal m'avise,
Jusqu'à tant que je soye de cest monde hors mise."

Adonc l'ame dévote est d'aimer plus fervente, 73
Tout le sens li deffault et le corps s'agravente,
A paines poeut parler mais le désir augmente,
Sur son lit se couche langoureuse et dolente.

Quant elle a les conduis de la gorge quassez, 74
De la langue palpite le son en est passés,
Si rent pleurs pour paroles largement et assez,
En plourant son seigneur qui pour luy fust lassés.

A l'ame langoureuse n'est rien qui puist souffire, 75
Fors quant pleure et gémist et largement souspire;
Son soulas et sa joye est quant du coeur remire
Les playes Jhesus Christ et son honteux martire.

Tout ainsi est ravy de celuy le coraige, 76
Qui voit son créateur morir pour son outraige;
Ne de la croix Jhésus ne retrait son visaige,
Car là ou est le coeur là est l'oeul par usage.

Larmes et griefs, souspirs, pleurs, et gémissemens 77
Li tournent en délices et en nourrissemens;
Ad ce met le martire tout son entendement,
Car à son grief martire fait grant accroissement.

Since this cannot be, it is proper for me to choose   72
A new crucifixion, so that I may be acceptable to my lover;
When I realize my own wickedness, I desire to weep and
    groan
Until the very moment that I am released from this world."

Now the devout soul becomes all the more burning in her
    love;   73
She is almost out of her mind, and her body grows heavy;
As her desire increases she can scarcely speak;
Languishing and sorrowful, she lies down on her bed.

With the passages of her throat almost crushed,   74
With her tongue palpitating and the sound of her voice
    rising up,
She sends forth floods of tears instead of words,
As she weeps for her Lord who suffered so grievously for her.

There is nothing which can satisfy the languishing soul,   75
Except tears and groans and deep sighs,
Her only solace and joy is contemplating
The wounds of Jesus Christ and his shameful martyrdom.

Then this soul is completely filled with rapture,   76
When she sees her Creator dying for her own
    transgressions;
She cannot keep from gazing upon Jesus crucified,
For, as usual, where the eye rests, there is the heart.

Tears and sorrows, sighing, weeping, and groaning—   77
All these are changed into delightful sustenance,
And this martyr puts all her mind to these things,
For by dint of her grief, she increases the very martyrdom
    itself.

[87]

En cest estat refuse la terrienne sorte,   78
Et dist que le soulas du monde venin porte,
Mais à l'eure de nonne elle appert comme morte:
Le frain de la char ront la mort qui tant est forte.

Car quant il luy souvient de la doulce parole   79
Que Jhésus dist à nonne, quant la vye se déssole,
Tout l'esperit ly pleure, et si brait comme fole,
Et dist que ceste voix son coeur perche et affolle.

Or ne poeut plus porter la sayecte angoisseuse;   80
Si muert comme j'ay dit, mais de mort bien eureuse,
Car du chiel li oeuvre on la porte glorieuse,
Qui la fait de Jhésus estre amie et espeuse.

Pour chelle n'iert plus messe de requiem dicte;   81
Ains soit gaudeamus de la messe l'introite;
Cilz se moque de dieu et l'esglise despite
Qui prye pour martir selon la loy escripte.

O rose tant vermeille! Ame de dieu aimee!   82
O pierre précieuse! O lys de la valee!
A qui tousiours despleust mondain fait et pensee,
Ton issue fut saincte et ta mort honnouree.

Eureuse es qui as la gloire conpvoitye   83
Es bras de ton espous doulcement endormie,
Et a son esperit tant forment abrye,
Tu rechoips les baisiers de pardurable vye.

78.4 **char.** *Chart* in the MS.
79.1 **doulce parole.** Replaces the more specific Latin *consummatum est.*

In this grievous state, she renounces the earthly
    existence,   78
And holds all worldly comfort as poison.
But at Nones she seems almost dead,
For mighty death is breaking the bridle of the flesh.

For when she recalls the gentle words   79
Which Jesus uttered at Nones while his life was draining
    away,
Her whole spirit weeps and cries like one bereft of her
    senses,
Wailing that this voice is piercing her anguished heart.

Now she can no longer bear the cruel arrow,   80
And she dies, as I have said—but a happy death—
For the glorious gate of heaven opens for her,
And now she becomes the beloved and the bride of Jesus.

For this blessed soul there is no need of a requiem Mass; 81
Rather let it be the *Gaudeamus* of the Introit of the Mass;
Truly he who prays for a martyr, according to the strict rule,
Mocks both God and the Church.

O rose so crimson! Soul beloved of God,   82
O precious stone! O lily of the valley!
You who always disliked worldly thoughts and deeds,
Holy was your departure and honored your death.

Happy are you who have achieved the glory you desired, 83
And are now rocked sweetly to sleep in the arms of your
    spouse;
Safe in the shelter of his spirit,
You receive the kisses of everlasting life.

[89]

Estoupe donc, amie, de larmes le conduit,   84
Car de ton espérance rechoips tu jà le fruit,
Car cilz qui t'a mené par le monde et conduyt
Te donne un doulz baisier qui le coeur te déduyt.

Dy, di ame dévote, pourquoy plus plourroyes: 85
Tu as du chiel la gloire, à tort tu te plaindroyes;
Se plus voloyes avoir, certes tu ne porroyes:
Jhésus est tes amys: en luy sont toutes joyes.

Cy fineray mes vers que ne soye ennuyeux,   86
Car se dire voloye combien délicieux
Est l'estat de ceste ame et combien glorieux,
On diroit que seroye de mentir curieux.

Quoy que ly autre dyent, mi frere et amy chier,   87
Qui du nouvel martir veulz la vie enchercher,
Quant tu seras ytel voeulles Jhésus prier
Que le chant du martir il te voeulle enseigner.

Cy fine le traictiet
du Roussignol

87.4 te. By use of *te*, rather than *nous*, the French has unfortunately lost
the idea of intercession, which is quite clearly the point of the Latin
with its form *nos*.

Stop up the conduits of your tears, beloved,   84
For now you are enjoying the fruits of your hope,
Since the one who led and guided you through this world
Now gives you a sweet kiss which delights your heart.

Say, say, devout soul, why should you weep longer: 85
You have the glory of heaven, and you would be wrong to
    complain,
If indeed you should wish for more, you could by no means
    have it,
For Jesus is your lover, and in Him all joys are.

Here I shall end my poem, lest I become tedious,   86
Because even if I should wish to relate how delightful
And glorious is the state of this soul,
I should only be thought to be contriving deceitful fictions.

Whatever other people say, my brother and dear friend—   87
You who wish to learn of the life of this new martyr—
When you have become like her, pray to Jesus
To teach you to sing like this martyr.

Here ends the poem of
the Nightingale

[91]

Bibliography

Philomena praevia:

Peacham, John. *Philomena, A Poem by John Peckham.* Trans. William Dobell. London: Burns, Oates & Washbourne, 1924.

Philomena praevia. Ed. G. M. Dreves. Vol. 50 of *Analecta Hymnica*, 602-16.

Raby, F. J. E. "Philomena praevia temporis amoeni." In *Mélanges.* Ed. Joseph de Ghellinck. Gembloux: J. Duculot, 1951. II, 435-48.

Nightingale:

Chandler, Albert R. "The Nightingale in Greek and Latin Poetry," *Classical Journal,* 30 (1934), 78-84.

Graves, Robert. *The Greek Myths.* 2 vols. Baltimore: Penguin Books, 1955.

Kohler, R. " 'Oci, oci' als Nachtigallensang." *Zeitschrift für Romanische Philologie,* 8 (1884), 120-22.

Pauly-Wissowa. *Real-Encyclopädie der Classischen Altertumswissenschaft.*

Raby, F. J. E. "Philomena praevia temporis amoeni." In *Melanges.* Ed. Joseph de Ghellinck. Gembloux: J. Duculot, 1951. II, 435-48.

Shippey, Thomas Alan. "Listening to the Nightingale." *Comparative Literature,* 22 (1970), 46-60.

Wilhelm, J. J. *The Cruelest Month.* New Haven: Yale University Press, 1965. Especially pp. 89-93; 98-100.